"Weapo...

Weapons of Mass Instruction

"Bite-Sized Business Nuggets!"

By John Eric Jacobsen

Copr. JBP, Inc., 2014 – JohnEricJacobsen.com

"Weapons of Mass Instruction"

Dedication

I dedicate this book to all of the great people I've met in my seminars and workshops nationwide. I learned a lot from all of you.

Special Thanks

To all of the people who have inspired me throughout my life and career. It's been a long road, but the rewards and joy have changed my life and made me a better person.

Other Special Thanks

To all of my teachers, trainers, authors, motivators and mentors from whom I've amassed the following 30 years of information and insights: James Needham, Brian Tracy, Helen Francis, Ken Coscia, Milton Trachtenburg, Fred Pryor, Dr, Helga Rhode, Jose Silva, K. Paul Grivas, Mark Jacobsen, June Graham, Ron G - Thank You!

Very Special Note

This book is written in a conversational style and formatted in an instructional style. Much of the information was drawn from my live seminars or training.

John Eric Jacobsen
Jacobsen Business Seminars, Inc.
Copyright, 2014 JBP, Inc.
JohnEricJacobsen.com

It is **unlawful** to reprint, republish or redistribute any part of this book in part or in full without **written permission** from the author and publisher.

"Weapons of Mass Instruction"

Great Feedback

"Weapons of Mass Instruction is an incredible book for your business and personal life. It is a tasty mix containing wisdom, insight, and methodology for solving daily business problems that arise. I highly recommend this book to anyone working in any business or trade." – Mr. John Gigante, Shiloh Street Pictures, New York, NY

"What a great and necessary book for corporate America. This book has many nuggets and strategies for anyone in business, sales or customer service. What I was most impressed with was how much of the book applies to my personal life. This book is excellent and very easy to read. I recommend it to all of my clients." – Ms. Kathy Parrin, NFL Films

"Although I have read many business books, Weapon's is by far the best. No hype or psycho-babble that is so widespread today. I believe that Jacobsen's book will be around long after the others are gone. My brother works in a large east coast hospital, and Weapons of Mass Instruction is required reading for all management and customer service reps. The communication & conflict strategies are superb." – Mr. Grant Stilime, Stilime, Inc.

'*Weapons of Mass Instruction is not only an apt title, but it's also an incredibly intelligent book. I read this book while preparing for an interview for a better job. It strengthened my confidence, and I landed the job based on the communication principles I applied from this book. I recommend this book to everyone wanting to succeed. This book is a "Must-Read!"* – Mr. John Barbera, Buffalo, NY

"Without a doubt, a must-read book for any business professional. I recommend reading it with a highlighter." – Ms. Gen Korman, Rutherford, NJ

"Weapons of Mass Instruction"

Weapons of Mass Instruction focuses on the Top 6 Most Relevant Business Concerns and offers insights in a bite-sized format!

1. Success & Goal Achievement!
2. Customer Service Skills!
3. Corporate Wellness!
4. People Skills!
5. Communication Skills!
6. Conflict Resolution & Confrontation Skills!

Lessons to be Revealed

1. What you allow, you teach.
2. Building another's self-esteem is the pinnacle of people skills.
3. Goals are the key to personal and professional life mastery.
4. Common sense is not always common.
5. You can model successful behavior traits.

Table of Weapons

A Quick Introduction!	Page - 6
What a Duck Taught Me About Success!	Page – 7
Affirmations to Pump up Your Day!	Page - 10
Personal & Professional Goal Achievement!	Page - 13
Your Team Is Lazy because Your Goals Are Hazy!	Page - 20
While the Economy's a Bust Training is a Must!	Page - 23
25 HOT Networking Tips!	Page - 26
Dealing with Negative Customers & Remaining Up-Beat!	Page - 31
Dealing with Angry Customers!	Page - 35
Humanizing Customer Service!	Page - 39
5 Easy Steps for Telephone Mastery in Customer Service!	Page - 42
5 Ways to Build a Great Staff!	Page - 46
Spotting Personal or Employee Burn-Out!	Page - 49
Corporate Wellness and Meditation!	Page - 52
Corporate Wellness to Eliminate Habits!	Page - 55
Help Your Employees to Stop Smoking!	Page - 59

"Weapons of Mass Instruction"

Table of Weapons (continued)

Corporate Wellness and Walking!	Page - 64
Boost Your Productivity with Water!	Page - 68
Stress Management in the Workplace!	Page - 72
Dealing with Temper Tantrums in the Office!	Page - 77
Tips to Remain Calm During an Argument!	Page - 80
Dealing with Crying in the Workplace!	Page - 84
Please, Help! My Boss Is Hitting on Me!	Page - 87
The 6 Qualities of a Healthy Personality!	Page - 89
Dealing with Negative People!	Page - 92
The Magic of Conflict!	Page - 98
A New Concept – Win-Win-Heal!	Page - 101
When's the Best Time to Avoid Conflict?	Page - 106
When to Walk Away from a Conflict—And Not Look Back!	Page - 109
The 8 Primary Communication Bloopers!	Page - 113
Listening with Both Ears!	Page - 117
Characteristics of a Great Leader!	Page - 121
3 Power Steps for Becoming More Assertive!	Page - 125
3 Power Steps for Giving Constructive Criticism!	Page - 127
3 Power Steps for Responding to Criticism!	Page - 131
De-Clutter Yourself!	Page - 133
Business Advice from the Godfather!	Page - 137
Ye Olde Office Rules!	Page - 142
Two Seas of Palestine!	Page - 143
About the Author!	Page - 144

"Weapons of Mass Instruction"

A Nugget-Sized Introduction

For over three decades, I've been traveling our great country presenting my business and corporate training seminars. Each workshop participant receives a workbook to follow, which helps make the lesson delivery more efficient and memorable. I have to admit it; I love writing books and workshop manuals. I find it very relaxing sitting at my computer for a few hours or weeks compiling training information and placing it into workbook format. I find it very rewarding.

Popular demand was my motivation for writing this book. My seminar attendees are always calling our office wanting more information on specific topics and stating that I said something in class that *was not* in their workbook. Several companies I've worked with have gone far enough to video or audio record each training as if every word is a golden nugget. I must say it is gratifying.

Therefore, to answer the call and requests, this book is an actual transcript of some of my most requested topics taken from professional videos and audios made at many of my seminars. This book is creatively edited to remain in a *"bite-sized nugget format."* I've removed much of the fluff for convenience purposes, and only the nuggets remain--short, straightforward, content-rich and direct. Remember, the dictionary defines a "nugget' as a precious lump of gold having great worth and importance.

My goal is to *"arm"* you with these instructional weapons for refreshing your skills, and for sharing them with your co-workers. The outcome will produce a more harmonious work environment and greater human relations. I trust it to be a valuable guide in the resolution of particular *"soft-skill"* business or personal problems.

I know you'll find great benefit in these pages, and as always I wish you luck and success.

"Weapons of Mass Instruction"

Weapon # 1

What a Duck Taught Me About Success!

In a tiny village lived a wise old prophet. The prophet spent his last years sharing wisdom, answering questions and giving advice to the people in the village. The people respected and loved the prophet because his advice was always helpful, and his answers always precise.

One day a young boy from the village decided to trick the prophet by asking a question that would be impossible to answer. The boy found a small live duck, concealed it behind his back and slowly approached the prophet. In a mocking voice the boy asked, "Prophet, I hold a duck behind my back. Tell me; is the duck dead or alive?" The prophet paused for a moment and gazed into the boy's eyes. In a whisper, he responded, "If I say the duck is dead, you will show me its live body. If I say the duck is alive, you will quickly choke it, and then show me its dead body. Therefore, I tell you the duck is neither alive nor dead. The duck is whatever you decide it will be."

I heard that story many years ago, and it made a powerful impression on me. I love sharing it in my seminars. It reminded me that each of us has the power to decide our fate and destiny. For each of us, our potential for success is like the duck in this story.

"Your success will be whatever you decide it will be."

For many people, success is a very personal but subjective type of thing. I understand the personal part. However, the subjective part must be made objective or concrete so you can recognize your success when you arrive there. Without some objectivity as to what your success will feel, sound, taste, smell, and look like, you won't know when you've succeeded, or if you've already succeeded---unknowingly. It's similar to trying to kick a field goal without knowing where the goal post is. Simply put, you cannot be successful unless you first define and understand what success means to you.

"Weapons of Mass Instruction"

The dictionary defines "success" as the achievement of something desired, planned or attempted. Although that definition is accurate, it does not touch upon our visions. What are *your* measurements for success? What does success mean to you? How will you know whether you are or are not successful if you have not yet defined what success means to you? Do you know what must precisely happen in your life, job, career, marriage or business for you to feel successful?

Some people use money as a measuring stick for success. If they have an abundance of money, they consider themselves successful; if their finances are in shambles, they consider themselves failures. Others believe that if money is your only motive for success, then you are already a failure. Some people feel very successful if they own a new car or a large house. Others may live in a modest apartment and use public transportation and they, too, feel successful because they are content where they are. Someone else may feel successful if he or she is the president of a large corporation. Others may be happy and fulfilled working in the mail room. In Hollywood, you're considered successful if your name is in the gossip columns and not in the phone book.

To begin defining your version of success, you can start by asking yourself two important questions:

1. What must precisely happen in my life for me to feel successful and ultimately fulfilled?

2. How will I know when I have achieved it?

Stop now and write out your answers to these two questions. It may take some time and serious thought; however, they are the foundation for the rest of your life.

Answering these questions reveals your criteria. Remember, there are no right or wrong answers; your criteria is just a measurement of what is important to you and an analysis of your values. Compare those standards with your current life situation, and that assessment designates whether or not you're a success, or at

"Weapons of Mass Instruction"

least if you're on the right track. In my life, I feel fulfilled and satisfied when the following five areas are balanced:

1. I must have a happy family life by feeling connected to my wife and children.

2. I must experience physical, emotional and mental health with vibrant energy.

3. I must be engaged in a labor of love.

4. I must feel that I am serving others.

5. My business must be prosperous.

These "success posts" are my criteria for success. I strive to keep them always flourishing, and I'm happy to report that 85% of the time they are at the levels I desire. What could be more satisfying than knowing you are living up to the dream inside you? What could be more important than discovering your talents and developing them? What could be more fulfilling than doing what you love every day?

You were born to win! Success can be learned; it leaves clues, and it has a formula. These clues and formulas for success are alive *within* you.

"However, your definition of success or criteria must precede all of this."

The moment you choose, define and more importantly "crystallize" your vision, you will discover that it's much easier to arrive--- if you knew where you were going ahead of time. The duck is behind your back. What are you going to do with it; let it live or let it die?

Quote for Thought:

"I'm an overnight success, but it took 20 years." – Monty Hall

"Weapons of Mass Instruction"

Weapon # 2

Affirmations to Pump-Up Your Day!

I have a morning ritual to kick start my body and jump start my day; it's advantageous and takes about 10 minutes.

1. As soon as I open my eyes, I do a 2-3 minute meditation. In meditation, I visualize a precise blueprint of how I expect my day to turn out.
2. Then I drink an extra large glass of water on an empty stomach. Drinking water first thing in the morning energizes and purifies your internal system, along with many other therapeutic benefits.
3. For about 2 minutes I do some gentle stretches.
4. My final step is to enthusiastically and passionately repeat and shout out two of my favorite affirmations: *"Everyday in every way, I'm getting better and better,"* and *"I'm heading for something bigger and better, sooner than I think."* Both of which I learned from a dear friend, motivator, and mentor, Mr. James Needham.

Affirmations are a favorite technique used for programming your subconscious mind and vital tools for pumping-up your day. Affirmations are clear, concise, positive suggestions designed to influence your subconscious and create a particular outcome. Affirmations are said aloud with strong, sincere emotion and repetition.

"While they do not replace the necessary physical work required while trying to reach a goal; they are potent tools that can keep your energy, motivation, and enthusiasm high."

I am a true believer in the power of affirmations. People we admire for their success stories like Jim Carrey, Will Smith, Oprah Winfrey and Tony Robbins have used affirmations to better their lives. I've used affirmations every morning for most of my life to pump up my day and to keep me in the "power-zone."

"Weapons of Mass Instruction"

Affirmations have helped me to improve my attitude, improve my focus, and to reach many goals.

Affirmations are very similar to autosuggestion, which is a form of subconscious reprogramming made famous by Dr. Emile Coue'. Dr. Coue' coined the world-famous self-help affirmation, *"Every day in every way I am getting better and better!"*

Dr. Coue' believed that many of his patients' health problems were psychosomatic (suggesting a negative mind created the problem). Coue' also believed that if people could become psychosomatically ill, they could also become psychosomatically healthy by merely talking themselves into it.

His prescription for many of his patients was to repeat (dozens and dozens of times daily) the affirmation, *"Every day in every way I am getting better and better!"* Psychologically, like repeating a mantra or chanting, the endless repetition bores the conscious mind, causing the affirmation to slip effortlessly into the patient's subconscious. Once the affirmation was rooted in the subconscious, many of Dr. Coue's patients were indeed healed.

Although this affirmation is not a substitution for professional medical care, it often seems to aid in the healing process. If the patient is very open to the power of suggestion, it may correct the problem entirely.

Last year I worked with a woman in one of my classes who was plagued with a severe case of psoriasis. It covered most of her scalp with white, crusty flakes that would occasionally bleed, always itched, and made her feel very unattractive. She tried many kinds of medical treatments, including prescription shampoo, yet nothing seemed to help her. As she asked for my advice, I could see that she was very discouraged since she suffered from this challenge for several years. I told her that affirmations "may" help if she used them with consistency. After our short discussion, she began using affirmations every time she was in the shower. While washing her hair and gently massaging her scalp she would repeat, *"Clear, healthy*

"Weapons of Mass Instruction"

scalp," several times with emotion and sincerity. She said she began to notice some improvement in only two days. Finally, much to her amazement, the problem completely cleared up in one month and has not returned in over a year. You can begin using affirmations right now to pump up your day.

"Your affirmations must be short, positive and stated in the present tense."

Once you have selected one or several affirmations, repeat each of them often with strong, sincere emotion. You may repeat them aloud or while looking into a mirror. Your subconscious will absorb the command and help you to produce the results.

Here are some empowering positive affirmations to help you pump up your day. I've successfully used them all. However, use these as examples to assist you in creating your own.

* Every day, in every way, I am getting better and better!
* I am headed for something bigger and better sooner than I think!
* Today is going to be great!
* I feel fantastic and full of energy!
* I remain calm and relaxed in stressful situations!
* I will always maintain a perfectly healthy body, brain and mind!
* I get things done in a timely fashion!
* I am a peaceful, centered human being!

"Be sure to repeat your affirmations with strong, sincere emotion."

The attitude and emotional intensity you use while repeating your affirmations are critical. Your attitude sends a high alert signal to your brain, forcing your mind to place your affirmation on a priority status. This priority status helps to move you closer to your goals while keeping you pumped!

Quote for Thought:

"Affirmation without discipline is the beginning of delusion." – Jim Rohn

"Weapons of Mass Instruction"

Weapon # 3

Personal & Professional Goal Achievement!

A Story

I was taking a Sunday drive, and I stopped at a red light. While waiting for the light to turn green, I noticed a small vacant field across the way. A voice in the back of my head said, *"That would be a great location for an ice cream parlor."* About seven months later I found myself driving down the same road and stopped at the same red light. Much to my surprise, an ice cream parlor opened on that same vacant field. The parking lot was jammed, and it seemed to be doing great business. I began to wonder, how many other people stopped at that same light seven months ago? How many of them had the same idea or vision that I did? How many of them got the same intuitive message? But in the end, only one person took action--- and it wasn't me!

My Motivation

When it's my turn to make my transition from this world to the next, I want to be able to look back on my life and feel a sense of accomplishment and pride. I refuse to go to my grave with my music still in me. I want my life to be an example to my children that anything is possible.

How about you? What kind of legacy do you want to leave behind? How do you want to be remembered? Will you look back on your life and feel empty? Will you look back with joy and the pleasure of knowing you've reached your potential? Can you imagine the joy of fulfilling all of your dreams and completing your life's journey without regrets? Focusing on reasonable, compelling goals can help you realize your vision.

Your goals are your blueprints for the future. Goals are dreams about to be born. Goals are the ladders we climb to reach our vision of success. If you don't have goals, you end up working for someone who does have goals.

"Weapons of Mass Instruction"

"We all have within us everything we need to achieve and generate successful, happy, healthy lives. We possess the ability to realize all of our dreams. These powers are always within your reach."

The only requirement to obtain this power is to take action and use it. The moment you tap the power available to you, all of your goals will bow down to you. That is your birthright, ---so claim it now!

An Interesting Study

In 1953, Yale University conducted a study of their graduating seniors. The study determined that only 3% of the graduating class had clearly defined goals. Twenty years later, in 1973, the University did a follow-up study with the same members of the class of 1953 and discovered that the same 3% who had clearly defined goals were more successful in life than the other 97% combined. That is an astonishing report which proves that to get ahead in life we must have goals.

The Average Reality

The sad fact is that the average person spends more time planning their vacation than planning their lives. We spend more time planning the honeymoon than planning the marriage. The average American spends an average of seven hours a day watching TV or surfing the web. Worse, we play on facebook all day using it as an escape from our unhappy reality, and as a tool to create our own "reality show." If we'd only spend as much time for creative thinking as we do on moronic texting, we'd see an incredible shift in our success rate.

We've all fallen into this deep trance, and we spend most of our day caught up in the hypnosis of social conditioning. Is it any wonder why so few people succeed? We're too busy filling our minds with mental candy, instead of mental protein.

The fact is that human beings are "goal-seeking mechanisms." The excitement that pumps through your body when you are pursuing a worthwhile goal is exhilarating. That powerful energy keeps you alive and feeling young. As human beings, we are

"Weapons of Mass Instruction"

only truly happy when we are working towards the fulfillment of our desires. Happiness is a by-product of work and achievement.

"Goals are vitamins for your soul. It does not matter how small or large your goals may be. By following this 6-step formula, you will fulfill all your dreams and join the elite top 3%."

The 6 Step Goal Achievement Formula:

1. You Must Know What You Want!

That the first significant step in goal setting. You must know precisely what you want, and you must write it down. You must also be able to state your goal or intention in one short sentence or less. If you cannot state your goal in one short sentence or less, then you do not have clear, concise goals. If your goals are not specific, you will design a hazy, sloppy future and condemn yourself to a life of mediocrity.

What specific outcomes do you desire? What is your end result? You cannot reach your goals unless you know what they are. You must have a specific target to aim at. One of the most popular weekend vacations is the famous "Cruise to nowhere." This cruise has a very specific destination. The passengers realize that they are going to "nowhere" and then they'll return. Even "nowhere" is "somewhere" if that is what you're aiming for. Knowing this, you must aim your mind at a specific target before you can hit the bull's eye.

Specifically, write out all of your goals in a personal notebook, and review them regularly. For each of your goals, list at least ten benefits you will receive when the goal is accomplished. Then write out ten benefits for each of the first ten benefits. When you can do this, your desire will be super high. Review these benefits for several minutes in the morning and several minutes before retiring. You will then be pounding these benefits into your subconscious mind. Remember, a goal correctly set is halfway attained.

"Weapons of Mass Instruction"

2. Design a Flexible Plan and Follow It.

Once you have a specific goal in mind, your next step is to draw up a plan. The dictionary defines the word "plan" as a systematic method for accomplishing something. Planning is a tool that can help us to reach our goals. It is the vehicle that transports us from where we are to where we want to be. A good plan will keep you on the course and shorten the road to your goal. I have made many mistakes in my life by not creating practical plans. I was under the impression that I just needed to have a goal and then everything else would effortlessly fall into place. I fooled myself. Having a plan is a tool that will dramatically improve your goal achievement success rate.

Follow your plan precisely the way you designed it. If, during your journey, you decide to alter your plan, then do so. Flexibility is a key to success. Begin working steadily toward your dreams; you'll be amazed how fast your ship will come in if you swim out to meet it with a plan.

3. Identify Any Obstacles and How to Avoid Them.

By reviewing, discovering or forecasting any obstacles you may encounter on the goal achievement road, you will be better prepared to avoid them. That is positive thinking at its finest. Reach out to people who can assist you in overcoming those obstacles, and use them as mentors. Model their behaviors and strategic thinking skills to rise above the foreseen difficulties. If you must--- ask them for a piggyback ride, or better yet to stand on their shoulders. Personally, I've left my footprint on many people's shoulders, and I never have a problem admitting it, or giving those wonderful mentors credit.

"Weapons of Mass Instruction"

4. Use Positive Affirmations Daily for Reinforcement Purposes.

We discussed this strategy in weapon 2, but it's worth repeating. Affirmations are a popular technique used for programming your subconscious mind. Your affirmations must be clear, concise, positive suggestions designed to influence your subconscious and motivate you to reach your goals. **Remember,** they do not replace the necessary physical work required while trying to achieve a goal; they are potent tools that can keep your driving force & enthusiasm high.

5. Keep Your Goals a Secret & Avoid Vampires!

The easiest person to find on this Earth is someone who will tell you *"You won't succeed; it can't be done, or I tried that, and it didn't work."* Anyone who discourages you from your dreams is called a "vampire." These people suck the energy out of you by shedding negativity on your dreams. You'll be surprised how many people will be threatened by your success. It is written in the New Testament to *"Go forth and tell no one,"* and *"Do not tell your left hand what your right-hand does."* Whatever your religious beliefs, the wisdom in these writings teaches us to SHUT UP! Keep your dreams and goals a secret. Do not tell anyone what lies ahead in your future. Envy does strange things to people. Sadly, as you climb the ladder of excellence, you will discover who your real friends are. Share your dreams and goals only with like-minded people.

"Share your dreams and goals only with people who will support and assist you. These people are success-minded, and they will hold the ladder steady for you as you climb."

Surround yourself only with winners. Be like the customer who went into the restaurant and ordered lobster. When the waiter delivered the lobster to the table, the customer noticed that the lobster's large front claw was missing. The customer asked, *"What happened to this lobster's front claw?"* The waiter responded, *"He lost it in a fight."* The customer demanded, *"Bring me the winner! I'll only eat the winner!"*

"Weapons of Mass Instruction"

Like this customer, associate only with the winners. Keep your goals a secret. It is easier to attain the mastery level when you have positive support from others. As for the negative vampires, let them see your dreams after they materialize, not before. I find it very interesting that most recently the world is so highly interested in vampire movies and TV shows. Perhaps it's because it's something we subconsciously recognize about ourselves.

6. Persist, Persist & Never Give Up!

When you have faith and a positive mental attitude, you realize that a so-called "failure" is only a different result or a delayed success. Failure is a precious lesson that teaches us to try a different road. Failure gives us the opportunity to alter our plans and to discover a better way. High achievers profit by their mistakes. When you study the lives of successful people, you will learn they have dozens of failures in their portfolio. That would put us in good company. People on the road to excellence expect occasional setbacks, yet they always pick themselves up --- persist and keep dancing.

Persistence is what makes a person a winner. Persistence gives a person the power to hold on when the road is rough, the ability to meet every obstacle, smile, and move on. Usually, when defeat overtakes a person, they will quickly retreat. That is one of the reasons why the bottom of the success ladder is very crowded. Success only releases its rewards and shines its beautiful face when a person refuses to quit. You must be willing to gamble all that you have to get through the door leading to victory. Persistence helps us to stack the odds in our favor. As you journey toward the realization of your dreams; make failure your teacher, not your undertaker.

Remember: If you plan to be an "overnight success," I guarantee that you'll be destroyed by morning. You will not have earned the "resiliency" or the "staying power" which winners have developed by being lucky enough to fail.

"Weapons of Mass Instruction"

Let's Remember:

1. You must know what you want with a definite purpose.
2. Design a flexible plan and implement it.
3. Identify and clarify any obstacles and how to avoid them.
4. Use passionate affirmations to keep you motivated.
5. Keep your goals a secret.
6. Avoid vampires.
7. Persist and never give up!
8. View perceived failures as gifts and opportunities.

A Parable

There was once a massive, ornate door. It was constructed of pure gold and priceless diamonds. Inscribed on the center of the door in bright, large letters was the word "Success." The door to success confused millions of people because it had no doorknob or handle to allow a smooth entrance. People tried to push it open, pry it open, kick it open, smash it in, and break it down. Some gave their lives to get the door to open. Despite all their efforts, the door only opened for a few.

The Nugget - It's easy to walk through the door of success once you realize the knob is on the inside within you.

"Weapons of Mass Instruction"

Weapon # 4

Your Team Is Lazy because Your Goals Are Hazy!

As a team leader your role is to understand and accomplish six key points:

1. Your job is to get the best out of each team member *individually* by keeping them focused and motivated.
2. Your job is to get the best out of your team as a *unit* by keeping them focused and motivated.
3. You must provide and support your team's vision.
4. You must maintain the motivational and inspirational health of your team.
5. You must be a mediator during conflict.
6. You must keep your team focused and progressing toward clearly stated goals and objectives.

The # 1 reason that teams fail is because of shabby goals. Without crystal, clear goals a team cannot function because it has no direction. When a team has no path, it's impossible for its members to give a full or complete commitment. It's also impossible for a team to know where it's going or how to get there without a shared vision. A shared vision is a key to keeping your team focused and motivated.

To properly accomplish corporate objectives, your team must work together as a finely tuned unit. The entire team must know exactly where they are going, how they will get there, and the exact steps required to complete the tasks at hand.

Here are three powerful, time-tested steps that will get your team up and running in no time. I believe that every corporate and business structure must have the following ideas deeply integrated into their foundations. Many companies worldwide have called these steps a **"Prescription for Success."**

"Weapons of Mass Instruction"

Step 1- Create a Team Vision Statement.

Your "vision statement" merely expresses where your team is going. Your vision statement must challenge its members to reach for higher ground, it must reflect your organization's core values, and all the members must easily understand it of the team. The vision statement is a verbal and written reflection of your team's "preferred future state." The vision statement for my company is that *"People and businesses are using our information to enhance their business and the quality of their lives."*

Step 2- Create a Team Mission Statement.

There is a significant difference between a vision statement and a mission statement.

1. A **vision statement** expresses where your team is going.
2. A **mission statement** reflects how your team will attain the vision.

For a mission statement to be effective, as with a vision statement, it must contain several indispensable components. Whereas a vision statement reflects the vision of your organization, a mission statement must reflect your team's core purpose. However, it must still support and exemplify the vision of your organization, or it will be weak. It must incorporate and integrate all departments and their functions. It must challenge your team to reach for higher ground, yet it must be attainable. When I combine the vision and mission statements for my company, it reads like this: *"To provide information and education in an entertaining format to enhance the quality of our client's business and personal lives."*

Whenever I visit a company, it never surprises me when the most successful businesses have their vision and mission statements framed and posted throughout the building. They serve as a ringing reminder for your team to remain focused and remember the purpose of their employment.

"Weapons of Mass Instruction"

Step 3- Establish Team Goals.

As discussed in weapon # 3, goals are essential for your team's success because they provide your team with a practical plan for moving forward. Your goals must state tasks, assignments, functions, responsibilities, timelines, schedules, and follow-up. Your team will flourish quicker if the goals are specific, attainable, and have a deadline attached. Be sure you assign each goal to the team member most equipped to reach the goal at hand, and you'll be moving at warp speed in no time at all.

Here are some Questions:

1. What's your team's vision?
2. Is it understood?
3. What's your team's mission?
4. Is it understood?
5. Do your vision and mission reflect your team's purpose?
6. Is it practical and attainable?
7. Can each team member recite from memory your vision and mission statements?

Let's Remember:

1. Create a team vision statement framed in the vision of your organization.
2. Create a team mission statement.
3. Your vision is where you're going; your mission is how you'll get there.
4. Establish team goals.
5. Be sure you assign each goal to the team member most equipped to reach the target at hand.

Quote for Thought:

"It's hard to beat a team that never gives up." - Babe Ruth

"Weapons of Mass Instruction"

Weapon # 5

While the Economy's a Bust Training is a Must!

Did you know that one of the first things to get slashed when corporate budgets get tight is employee training? That is an unfortunate reality. It reminds me of throwing the baby out with the bath water. Here at Jacobsen Business Seminars, Inc., we believe that trained employees are precisely what a company needs in lean times. My research demonstrates that training creates at least four essential benefits:

1. Training gets employees motivated and energized!

2. Training helps to stimulate employee creativity and growth!

3. Training creates higher employee morale with positive attitudes!

4. Training enhances communication and problem-solving!

Too many managers mistakenly view training as a luxury. However, in today's business culture training is a competitive and strategic necessity. *"What if we train our employees and they leave?"* they ask. Well, what if you don't train them and they stay? Here are three reasons why employee training is so necessary:

1. O.F.D.

"Originality, Flexibility and Determination" are required for building prosperous companies. O.F.D. comes from well-trained employees.

    A. **Originality** is born out of creativity.
    B. **Flexibility** is born by thinking out of the box.
    C. **Determination** is born from the strength of mind.

Training opportunities are a superb way to encourage and develop O.F.D. in the individuals in your workforce. Moreover, as your employees develop these new skills, they will develop leadership personalities. Your work environment will then

"Weapons of Mass Instruction"

become flooded with high energy levels and exceptional resourcefulness. O.F.D. are commodities crucial for keeping your company ahead of the competition. Also, learning new skills and interacting with other people has a direct impact on the productivity and development of your work environment.

2. Inspiration.

Inspiration is the foundation of creativity. Since training is a fundamental element for igniting creativity, your employees will be inspired with new ideas and creative strategies for solving old problems. Sometimes a "sensational new idea" is just an old idea with its sleeves rolled up. Inspiration is the tool that allows your employees to view problems in a different light. That is why inspiration is one of the most significant forces in the world. The mind stretched by inspiration never returns to its original dimensions.

3. Encouragement.

I have found that training encourages employees to learn all they can about the company--not just the department in which they work. I believe that providing employees with information about HR, shipping, accounting, production, marketing, or other aspects of the business gives your employees an excellent overall understanding of how all the pieces fit together, and how their part contributes to the whole. Sometimes, just removing your employees from the grind of their everyday work schedule is enough to jump-start their energy levels, while encouraging employees to recommit to their jobs.

Remember, training does not need to be expensive or last many days to be worthwhile or productive. I have found that workshops, mini-seminars and "lunch & learns" can be just as invigorating as the expensive courses and conferences.

I believe it is a great idea to begin implementing regular training programs for your employees. Training sessions held weekly, or monthly can be quite productive. You'll be giving your employees something outside the ordinary workday to look

"Weapons of Mass Instruction"

forward to, and encouraging a commitment to professional development and the enhancement of skills.

While a dedication to keeping training opportunities alive and thriving within your company may be an expense (including time and resources), the benefit regarding qualified and energetic personnel is well worth it. As a reminder, training is always paid for in one of two ways:

First – You pay for training!

Second – You pay for not training!

Let's Remember:

1. O.F.D!
2. Inspiration!
3. Encouragement!

Quote for Thought:

"Practice is the hardest part of learning, and training is the essence of transformation."
— Ann Voskamp, One Thousand Gifts: A Dare to Live Fully Right Where You Are.

"Weapons of Mass Instruction"

Weapon # 6

25 HOT Networking Tips!

Networking is a crucial ingredient for your business success. Whether you're involved in social media or live interactions, you must master this critical art to survive and surpass your competition. This particular weapon will focus on strategies for networking with live interactions.

Whether you're networking a small meeting, large meetings, social events, conferences, luncheons, trade shows, fundraisers, sports events, or your local chamber of commerce, the primary goal of networking is to meet people with the possibility of doing business together in the future. I've been networking throughout my entire business career. I find it a lot of fun meeting new people, finding common ground, and trying to make a connection. However, I've also had times when my networking experiences were tiresome and hectic. I truly value my time and did not want to waste it by attending a networking event and coming up empty-handed.

The following **HOT** networking tips are for you. After years of networking trial and error, I've utilized the following strategies to make good first impressions, meet the right people, and follow-thru with follow-up. It's critical for you to "shine" at networking events because you only have a few seconds to impress a possible future client or prospect, so you want to do it right the first time--- every time. I know these 25 tips will help you to perfect your networking talents. Naturally, the more events you attend, the faster you'll polish your skills.

1. **Arrival Time:** I always like to arrive at an event 10 minutes early. That gives me time to meet the people in charge, and they usually introduce me to other important people before the event begins. It also allows me the opportunity to check out the room and start remembering names.

"Weapons of Mass Instruction"

2. **Your Attire:** The manner in which you dress is critical; it helps to create an excellent first impression. Clean, casual business attire is expected. No distasteful or revealing clothing EVER! Be sure all your zippers are zipped! Polished shoes, clean teeth, fresh breath, neat hair, and clean nails. (Don't take this lightly!)

3. **Cell Phones:** Put your cell phone on vibrate!

4. **Your Entrance:** Always walk in the room, and observe first. Inconspicuously scan the room to see who you would like to meet or connect with. Remember everyone else is doing the same, so be prepared to make a great first impression.

5. **Approaching People:** When deciding on a person to meet, I always try to approach someone who is alone or not speaking with anyone. Walk up to that person, glance at their name tag, and introduce yourself using that person's name. Always present yourself in a pleasant, friendly way, and always smile. Be warm, sincere, and have a sense of humor. Establish an honest rapport upon which you can build a relationship. During your conversation try to offer information that they may find valuable. The first impression is crucial as people will form an opinion of you in the first few seconds--- so make it count.

6. **Name Tags:** At some networking events you may be expected to wear a name tag. If this is the case, remember always to wear your tag on your right side. That is because both of you will use your right hands to shake, and as a result, the eyesight of each party is automatically directed to the side the tag is on. It merely makes it easier for them to read your name tag.

7. **Introductions:** Remain courteous to those introducing themselves to you by listening to them. That can help you to remember their names. Shake their hand correctly, and give them good, respectful eye contact.

"Weapons of Mass Instruction"

8. **Alcohol:** Some networking events serve alcohol. That can be very tricky! If you do drink alcohol, drink in moderation---or less than that. Intoxication, slurring your words, alcohol breath, vomiting, and the inability to stand while at a networking event are not acceptable behaviors.

9. **DON'T SMOKE!**

10. **Misrepresentation:** Never misrepresent yourself or your company. The words you speak must always be honest and served with integrity.

11. **Respect & Courtesy:** Treat everyone you meet (including your competition) with respect, dignity, and courtesy. Never engage in any slanderous comments about anyone. Show respect and courtesy towards your competitors.

12. **Privacy:** Consider and respect other guests right to privacy and confidentiality. Never talk about confidential or private matters with anyone.

13. **Expert Opinions:** Respect the expert opinion of others in their area of proficiency. Never depreciate other guests.

14. **Sharing Information:** The networking event is about meeting people, making connections, and getting to know each other through the exchange of information. The most valuable information to share is about your business or company.

15. **Cursing:** Be very cautious of foul language, even if others are being offensive or abusive. Someone will overhear you, and it will cost you big time. The same goes for dirty or off-color jokes.

16. **Be Positive:** Always project a positive attitude. People will always remember your positive enthusiasm. It is also human nature to want to associate with positive people. Negative people are downers and usually not welcomed at networking events.

17. **Bragging:** Try to avoid tooting your own horn.

"Weapons of Mass Instruction"

18. **No Selling:** Networking is a time to meet new people and begin the process of building a relationship. With this in mind, remember it's not a place to start selling. You should only be selling yourself.

19. **Harassment:** Be aware of sexual harassment. Also, avoid sexual innuendos or pressuring people for dates. You may never get invited back, and it can cost you your job. I've seen this happen several times to intoxicated attendees.

20. **Clicking:** Understand and accept that you will not click with everybody, so don't waste your time with people who seem to "reject" you. Move on to those who exhibit a friendlier behavior.

21. **Never Interrupt:** If a person you previously met is involved in a discussion, and you would like to get re-acquainted, never interrupt. It is rude and will not be appreciated. I usually find someone else for the moment, or I approach the party of interest while remaining several feet away. If the party notices me and realizes I wish to rejoin the group, I courteously signal that I'll wait until they are finished speaking. You may try and join a group, or party caught up in a discussion, but your approach must be considerate of others in that group. Similarly, if you are in a group and another person would like to join--- invite them in.

22. **Business Cards:** Always bring your business cards and exchange them only after you have established rapport with someone. Business cards will soon be extinct but bring them regardless. Today, when people make contact they quickly connect at the event on LinkedIn or their cell phone.

23. **Write Notes:** When receiving a business card from someone, take the time to read it before putting it away. When you part ways, write important notes on the back of their card that can help you remember important points discussed & re-establish rapport after the event.

24. **Follow-Up! Follow-Up! Follow-Up:** Attending a networking event is only the beginning, now you must begin to develop the relationship. Perhaps you can start by sending them a small thank you card or note. Simply thank them for the

"Weapons of Mass Instruction"

courtesy they offered during the event you attended. The "ideal" thank you card or note is always handwritten, unless you have terrible handwriting. Of course, you can always send a short-email instead. Also, call them shortly afterward and continue nurturing the relationship. Never stalk people!

25. **It Never Ends:** Networking is an ongoing process; it never ends. However, when you do it properly your business will thrive.

I wish you luck as you continue to network your way to success and business prosperity. As I mentioned earlier, you may experience some trial and error on the networking highway, but it will get easier and more comfortable. The most important thing to remember is to attend as many events as possible, get recognized and HAVE FUN!

Quote for Thought:

"If it's the Psychic Network, why do they need a telephone number?" – Robin Williams

"Weapons of Mass Instruction"

Weapon # 7

Dealing with Negative Customers & Remaining Up-Beat!

It's no secret that dealing with the public can be a very challenging job. Unhappy or dissatisfied customers can ruin your entire day and create massive amounts of unnecessary stress.

Unfortunately, there is no magic formula to please every single person all of the time. However, there are several things you can do to help keep yourself upbeat and positive while you're swimming in a sea of negativity. I teach my students in all of my seminars that the employee who can keep their mouth closed is the employee who stays employed.

Listed below are ten steps that you can apply throughout the day to maintain your composure in adverse situations. I know you'll find them useful and please, share them with friends or co-workers.

1. Always visualize a large $ stamped on your customer's forehead if they are unhappy.

That will help you to remember that your client is paying your bills and feeding your family, and the outcome of this interaction may or may not cost you your job. Remember, a happy customer equals your paycheck.

2. Skip the news before work. Listen to soothing music or motivational information on your commute.

How you spend the first couple of minutes of your day usually predicts how the rest of the day will unfold. Therefore, skip the news if possible. The news is always full of negativity. It's always better to listen to pleasant, relaxing music or motivational CDs before you begin your day. These will fill your mind with the required positive motivation to help you tackle any problem person or situation.

"Weapons of Mass Instruction"

3. Always challenge yourself to find something to like about every customer.

While this may seem difficult, if you try hard enough, you can find something to like about everyone you come in contact with, even if it's the color of their clothes. During an encounter with this person keep your focus on the 5% you like about them, and your attention off the 95% you dislike.

4. Use Daily Affirmations to support yourself, such as:

* *"I'm doing the best I can!"*

* *"I am a winner!"*

* *"I trust myself!"*

* *"I can handle any problem!"*

* *"I like myself!"*

* *"I deserve this job!"*

As we discussed in weapon # 2, repeating positive affirmations has become a precious tool not only in the workplace but in the clinical and medical fields. Just like listening to motivational CDs, affirmations will fill your mind with positive messages helping you to tackle any problem person or situation efficiently. Affirmations help keep your mind focused on a future positive outcome rather than the negative situation at hand.

5. Always reward yourself for a job well done.

When you've had a lucky day, or if you successfully made it through a stressful day, it's important to pat yourself on the back. You deserve it--- don't you? After a tough week or month spend more time with family or friends. Go out for dinner or get a massage. These are very excellent ways to demonstrate self-appreciation.

"Weapons of Mass Instruction"

6. Keep a Glory File of thank you letters and every compliment you receive and review it often.

If you happen to receive thank you notes and compliments, a "Glory File" is an excellent idea. You can review it during a tough week, and it can serve as a "pick-me-up." A glory file can help you feel better about yourself if you're feeling down. It can remind you that you are appreciated and give you the motivation to keep going.

7. Avoid gossiping about negative customers.

Gossiping about negative customers will only intensify your anger and negativity. The gossip causes you to relive the negative experience as if it's still happening. That will cause your stress levels to rise and your productivity to falter. It's essential to master the skill of letting the negativity go as soon as the customer leaves your space. If not, that customer will own and control your power. *"You've sold your soul to the client without making a profit!"*

8. Avoid complainers, criticizers, and gossips in your office.

At a recent seminar, a participant told me that if he avoided all the complainers, criticizers, and gossips in the office, he would have no one to speak to. Regardless, as mentioned in numbers 2 & 4, this type of negativity fills your mind with emotions that will cause your behavior and productivity to falter. You're also associating with a group that never rises higher than their current position. "Birds of a feather flock together." Be an eagle!

9. Make a list of reasons you must appreciate your customers and thank them.
"Thank you for paying my salary."
"Thank you for helping me pay my mortgage."
"Thank you for helping me put food on my table."
"Thank you for my new car."
"I appreciate you giving me the privilege of serving you."

"Weapons of Mass Instruction"

"I feel lucky, honored, and blessed to have a job at all."
"Thank you for choosing me to do your business with."

Most of all, never for one minute believe that your employer pays you. Your company only supplies the check; your customer fills in the blanks. Be grateful to them.

10. List 20 things you're grateful for in your personal and business life and review it often.

If you're involved in a very stressful career, review your grateful list often. Similar to the aforementioned glory file, a grateful list can serve as a reminder as to why you've chosen this career. A gratitude list will remind you of the good things you have, and change your state from stressful to resourceful. Gratitude is not only the greatest of virtues but the parent of all the others. If you forget the language of gratitude, you can never be on speaking terms with happiness. Therefore, if you can't be grateful for what you have, at least be grateful for what you've escaped.

Remember, you will be dealing with crazy people all of your life. It's important to perfect your coping skills now, and then the pressure will affect you less and less. Eventually, you will be able to rise above it all, and the crazies will leave you feeling indifferent and calm.

Quote for Thought:

"Your most unhappy customers are your greatest source of learning." - Bill Gates

"Weapons of Mass Instruction"

Weapon # 8

Dealing with Angry Customers!

If you're a customer service rep (CSR), I'm sure you've had the pleasure of dealing with an irate customer. They storm into your place of business or on the phone as angry and miserable as a bear with constipation. In some instances, despite your best efforts, the customer may be very dissatisfied and merely wants to complain, scream and vent.

Regardless, if they barge into your workplace like Satan with a score to settle, or if they are screaming or yelling, if their face is red, their blood pressure is boiling, and you can see their fangs; apply the following steps:

Step1. Take them off the Floor Quickly.

It's essential to escort the irate to a place where your other customers cannot hear what's happening. That situation can create a more significant unnecessary disturbance. Once you have the customer in a private area, let them vent and complain as much as they want, and do not interrupt them. **Never, ever interrupt an irate.** It's important to remember that sometimes people just want to be heard. They need someone to listen to them. Although it may not always be pleasant, as a CSR, that is our job. **While they are venting, I always recommend that you imagine they are a loved one or an extraordinary friend.** This simple mind shift can help you stay calm in a highly charged situation. Your job is NOT to win an argument with them. Your job is to make them happy and keep them loyal so that you can continue getting paid.

Step 2. Be Professional and Empathetic.

In other words, put yourself in their shoes. However, do not allow yourself to get drawn into their anger or begin to take their negativity personally. The manner in which to do this is to remain detached from their personality and keep all of your focus on the issue and solution. The more you focus on your angry customer's personality, the more likely it will be for you to lose your cool. The greater your focus on a positive outcome the less likely you are to be distracted by negativity.

Step 3. Take Notes! (If possible.)

In some situations, it may be helpful to take notes. This strategy will force the customer to slow down their angry, fast-paced ranting so that you can catch up with your much slower note taking.

Step 4. Drop Your Voice.

Finally, when it's your turn to speak, soften your voice and speak in an even, conversational tone. Keeping your voice at a low volume can cause the person to calm down faster, giving you greater control.

Step 5. Apologize! (If necessary.)

Once the problem is resolved, it is crucial that you offer a sincere apology. Apologizing demonstrates your deep "understanding and empathy."

A Professional Apology also Consists of 5 Steps:

Step 1. Sincerely say, "I'm sorry."
Step 2. Honestly, ask for forgiveness.
Step 3. Assure your client that you will take every measure to prevent the problem from occurring again.
Step 4. (If necessary) Ask the customer if you can somehow make it up to them.
Step 5. After a few days, send them a note to apologize again or give a follow-up phone call. Many professional circles consider an email very appropriate. I believe a phone call adds a powerful personal touch.

"Weapons of Mass Instruction"

Two Important Points:

1. Step 4 in a professional apology is an optional step and usually applied only if your blunder was massive.
2. Step 5 in a professional apology is a very valuable tool to build rapport and honorability. Many businesses feel it's unnecessary, however, I believe it's an essential extra step toward building essential human relations.

In a recent customer service seminar, I was asked, *"What can I do if the client is wrong?"* In other words, while dealing with a disgruntled customer, you both realize that the mistake or blunder was the fault of the client from the very beginning. How can we respond in that situation?

I've been there many times, and I must repeat what I've been saying all along. Regardless of where the responsibility lies, treat them as you would your mother or father, brother or sister, son or daughter. Treat them like family.

As a good CSR, your only response must be to "save their face." Do not rub their noses in it. You will not score any points by proving your customer wrong, or by making them feels dim-witted. Since your client is the reason you have a job, you'll want to avoid squabbling or bickering with them. Remember, your job is not to win fights, but to win loyal friends. Instead, go out of your way to make them look good regardless. Saying things such as, *"It could happen to anyone,"* or, *"I've made the same mistake many times,"* can be a real rapport builder.

The words you choose in a situation such as this can destroy or repair a client's perception of who you are. Your words can also help you create a profound emotional connection with your customer. So choose your words and how you convey them very carefully. That is the focal point of all human relations. That will give you the mark of distinction, and your client will remain loyal to you and your company.

"Weapons of Mass Instruction"

Our customers might not always be right, but they are still our customers. More importantly--- they are **feeding your family**. So the next time you deal with an angry client ask yourself, *"Do I want to eat or be right?"*

Let's Remember:

1. Get angry customers off the floor as soon as possible.
2. Never interrupt an irate.
3. When it's your turn to speak—soften your voice.
4. Be professional and empathetic.
5. Take notes.
6. Apologize.
7. Follow up with a note, email, or phone call.

Quote for Thought:

"Well done is better than well said." - Benjamin Franklin

"Weapons of Mass Instruction"

Weapon # 9

Humanizing Customer Service!

Honestly, as a consumer are you seeing an increase or decrease in American customer service? Are the businesses you patronize doing all they can to maintain your business and keep you loyal? If you're dealing with a company on the phone do they sound sincere or are they just reading from a script? Here are two more questions: Why do they need a script to remember basic human relation skills? Why do some customer service reps act and speak as if they are Snooki or Kardashian wannabes?

My biggest complaint about today's customer service experience is that the people sound so forced and rehearsed. If you're not waiting endlessly for an annoying phone prompt, you end up speaking to a poorly rehearsed human automaton. Unfortunately, we live in a world where our technology has surpassed our humanity. Our customers and people, in general, are fed up with technology and are longing to get back to the basics. Customer service has to be about people again. Our clients deserve to be treated with a human touch and dignity. My prediction is that businesses of the future will not prosper because they have the "Midas touch" but because they have the "people touch."

Listed below are 16 actions that you can take right now to humanize your customers experience with your company. If after reading these nuggets you think they are over simplistic-- then you're right, they are! However, how many of your reps are using these tips on a regular basis, every day with every single customer?

How often do the basics get forgotten because they are "too basic?" How often are you reminding your reps about the importance of human relations skills? If you're interested in taking a step back to the basics, you'll find your business taking a giant advance to a level I call, **"Humanized Customer Service."**

"Weapons of Mass Instruction"

Very little explanation is necessary for these nuggets since they are genuinely about common sense. However, for your convenience, I have divided them into "Basic" and "Advanced" categories. I know they'll help.

The Basics:

1. Be polite, smile a lot, be kind and patient, sincerely treat them as if they are your best friend or relative. (Read that again, it's essential.)

2. Continuously address your customer by name. Learn to make small talk to help build the relationship and be an excellent listener.

3. Relish your interactions with all of your customers-even the grumpy ones. Make them feel as if they've found a second home. Be sure they leave the interaction feeling good about you, your company, and themselves.

Advanced:

4. Remember their children. Remember their names and birthdays.

5. Always ask for feedback or have a suggestion box. Remember, many fortunes have been made because of the nuggets our customers place in a small suggestion box.

6. Accept full responsibility for errors and admit your mistakes. Always be honest. You can't always be perfect, but you must always have integrity.

7. Always deliver when promised and maybe even sooner. Instead of making outlandish promises that you can't keep, focus on being reliable.

8. Tailor to fit their needs and find unmet needs.

9. Refer them to another company if you actually can't help them. (Remember the movie "Miracle on 34th Street.")

10. Invite them to special events - or visit them.

"Weapons of Mass Instruction"

11. Patronize their business or company for an added WOW!!!

12. Display or give out their business cards.

13. Eat the tax, or shipping, or handling fees for great customers--- if possible.

14. Send gifts or unique occasion cards such as anniversaries or birthdays.

15. Sincerely say, *"Thank you for bringing this problem to my attention,"* and thanking customers for allowing you to fix their problems, and most of all saying, *"Thank you for your business."*

16. Think "WIN-WIN" and you will "WIN-WIN!"

Quote for Thought:

"Spend a lot of time talking to customers face to face. You'd be amazed how many companies don't listen to their clients." - Ross Perot

"Weapons of Mass Instruction"

Weapon # 10

5 Easy Steps for Telephone Mastery in Customer Service!

It happened on March 10, 1876. Alexander Graham Bell summoned his assistant, Mr. Watson, to the next room--- by telephone. That was over 130 years ago, and since then billions of local and long distance phone calls have been made around our world.

The telephone has been a fantastic tool for personal use and for keeping people globally connected. However, in the business world, it may be the most essential tool of all. Professionally, you must learn to play your telephone as if you were playing an instrument in a finely tuned orchestra. Your phone skills are a critical part of your business success. Your customers and clients are critically judging your business savvy and judging "you as a person" by your telephone etiquette.

The same applies to your receptionist, your assistants, and your customer relations team. Their phone skills must be highly polished because they are your front-line people. These are the people your clients will have first and future contact with. This scenario can create a real "make it or break it" game for your company.

Listed below are five etiquettes and time-tested telephone strategies. They will help you and your team to shine. They will allow you to project a powerful and professional image to anyone you are dealing with over the phone. This professional projection is crucial for obtaining and keeping your customers.

Mastery Step 1 - Master Relaxing & Getting Focused!

The first step in telephone mastery is essential because this is where the first impression is created. When you pick up the phone, you must not sound rushed, confused or undependable. Therefore, it's important to take a deep breath, get centered and relax before you pick up. Your customer wants to hear someone who sounds focused, intelligent and eager to assist. Remember it takes less than five seconds for your client to formulate a first impression about you while on the

"Weapons of Mass Instruction"

telephone. Make sure you have no food in your mouth, spit out your gum and sound intelligently focused.

Mastery Step 2 - Master Answering Quickly!

Despite the fact that it's cheaper to install an answering system in your phone services; customers still prefer to talk to a live person. Personally, I dislike pressing 1, and then pressing 2, and then pressing 3, before I can speak to someone who can assist me. Regardless, industry standard tells us to answer our business phone within the 2nd or 3rd ring. That seems to be the professional standard. Believe it or not, answering on the very first ring may startle your client; while waiting for the 4th or 5th ring may annoy them, especially if they are already unhappy with your services. Always remember this crucial point: *"A customer will begin to mentally measure the quality of your organization before they hear the voice by the number of rings it takes to get an answer."*

Mastery Step 3 - Master a Professional Greeting!

There are four steps to a professional greeting. These steps will help convince your customer that they are dealing with a cutting-edge, polished establishment. Although the steps are simple, they are imperative on the business etiquette scale. They will help you to establish instant rapport and credibility with your customers. I call them **"The 4 Answering Courtesies."**

A. Greet your customers with Good Morning, Afternoon, or Evening; **NEVER** Hello! Hello is used in your home, not in your business.

B. Give them the company name.

C. Give them your name.

D. Then ask, *"May I help you?"*

"Weapons of Mass Instruction"

Here's a quick example. When we answer the phones at our company it sounds exactly like this: *"Good Morning, thank you for calling Jacobsen Business Seminars, this is John, May I help you?"*

Mastery Step 4 - Master Crystal, Clear Diction!

Although you may have learned the perfect greeting, it's critical that your diction is also excellent. There's nothing worse than calling a company, and you can't understand the person you are speaking with. Constantly having to ask a rep to repeat themselves is a massive inconvenience for a client, especially if you are trying to sell them something. Your customer must be able to understand every letter, syllable, and word that comes out of your mouth. You must not speak too fast or too slow. The standard rate of speech is about 125 words per minute. You must not talk too loud or too soft. Your pitch, speed, and volume should be at a moderate level and at the same time sounding pleasant, friendly and professional. Ideally, your tone and inflections should vary.

Mastery Step 5 - Master Courtesy!

Use your voice to create a courteous attitude. Use your voice to indicate your willingness and enthusiasm to help. Remember a tired voice lacking passion is very unappealing. Your voice must make the customer feel welcome. Put a smile in your voice. That is easily accomplished by actually smiling as you are speaking on the phone with your client. Believe me; they will sense your friendliness through the line. It may help you to tape the word "SMILE" on your receiver. However, this is the most crucial point of all: *"That your telephone voice and customer interaction must make your client feel as if they've come home."*

"Weapons of Mass Instruction"

Here are some Questions:

1. How long does it take for your reps to answer a customer call?
2. Do your reps have clear, understandable diction?
3. Do your reps speak too quickly or mumble?
4. Do your reps sound human, or like robots?
5. As a customer, would you feel comfortable calling your call center?
6. Do your reps answer the phone with a polished, professional greeting?

Let's Remember:

1. Master relaxing & getting focused.
2. Master answering quickly.
3. Master a professional greeting.
4. Master crystal, clear diction.
5. Master courtesy.

Quote for Thought:

"Old fashioned telephones used to have cranks on them---some still do!"~Rick Bertoldo

"Weapons of Mass Instruction"

Weapon # 11

5 Ways to Build a Great Staff!

Several years ago, I was very fortunate to spend some time with George T. Muller, former president of Subaru of America, Inc. During his 1993 - 2000 tenure as president of Subaru, Mr. Muller led a significant revamping of the organization and brand by focusing on its core strength which is "all-wheel-drive vehicles." Under his incredible leadership, Subaru had a dramatic revenue and profitability turnaround with sales more than tripling to the $4 billion level. He was a great visionary and a fascinating man.

We talked about creativity, problem-solving and ingenuity, but I was most impressed with the real love and respect he had for his team, people, staff, and co-workers. We both agreed that a loyal staff or team plays an integral part in building and maintaining a great company.

As a manager or owner, it's important to remember the key factors in the construction of a high-powered staff. They are quite literally your lifeblood and must be treated as such. By observing Mr. Muller and his interactions with his employees, I noticed he had several key people skills which I believe made him so successful. You can turn your staff into a team that does the best possible job for your organization by implementing these five ideas:

1. Be Approachable.

You must be friendly to your employees, however, do not treat them as close personal friends. The reality is that they want you to be the boss and they want to be the employees. You need to be someone they can converse with on multiple non-work-related topics. From sports to children's issues, from family to vacation plans. They must always feel safe and non-threatened while in your presence. An open door policy is always appreciated.

"Weapons of Mass Instruction"

2. Be Loyal.

If staff members know you're always loyal to them, they'll give you the same in return. That is called the "law of indirect effort." If you want to be heard, you must first listen. If you want to be appreciated, you must first appreciate. If you want to get recognition, you must first recognize. If you can't get what you need, help others get what they need. If you want a genuinely loyal staff, be a loyal manager. Sometimes to be genuinely faithful to another person you must be willing to allow your interests to take second place. The manager of the future will make decisions that are first best for the employees and the bottom line second. In the future, this type of mindset will help you climb the corporate ladder at an accelerated pace.

3. Be Reliable.

Be a person who consistently does as promised and you will be known as reliable. Reliability is an admirable social character trait, and it's a standard feature in great leaders. When you hire people you expect them to be reliable, just be sure you demonstrate the same courtesy. Be aware that when it comes to demonstrating reliability, never listen to what people say, instead watch what they do. Actions always speak louder than words.

4. Be Fair.

That is the fastest way to establish your credibility among your employees. When dealing with people and problem solving you must be free from bias and judgment. You must be willing and open to see all points of view before making decisions. Be ready to put yourself on the line and go to bat for your staff. Also, be prepared to walk the trenches and get your feet wet with them. That is another common trait among great leaders.

"Weapons of Mass Instruction"

5. Have Fun with Your Employees.

Never be too busy to laugh or tell a joke. A good laugh helps people to shine through a crisis, and when your manager is laughing with you, it can indeed lift spirits. I'm not asking you to be a comic or clown; just don't be Mr. or Ms. Dull head.

Here are some Questions:

1. Does your staff respect you?
2. Does your staff like you?
3. Would your staff say you were a reliable and fair person?
4. If you took a position elsewhere, would your employees want to follow you?
5. Would you want to work with you--- or for you?
6. If the entire world treated each other in the same manner you treat your employees or staff, what kind of world would it be?

Let's Remember:

1. Be approachable.
2. Be loyal.
3. Be reliable.
4. Be fair.
5. Have fun with your employees.

Quote for Thought:

"Outstanding leaders go out of their way to boost the self-esteem of their staff. If people believe in themselves, it's amazing what they can accomplish." – Sam Walton

"Weapons of Mass Instruction"

Weapon # 12

Spotting Personal or Employee Burn-Out!

Burnout is a state of emotional, mental, and physical exhaustion caused by excessive and prolonged stress. Job burnout is the dread and lack of motivation for going to work. Sadly, if not caught in time and corrected, burn-out can spread to every area of your life. Everyone is susceptible to burn-out; there are no exceptions. My research shows that it is scarce for someone to suffer from burnout on the job, yet be happy and enthusiastic at home. Burn-out usually starts small like a tiny flame, but if left unattended it can quickly spread and destroy like a forest fire.

The differences between stress and burnout are interesting. Stress is a tremendous amount of physical pressure, while burn-out is associated with mental and emotional symptoms. However, I have worked with some people who were so stressed out they were not able to recognize they were also suffering from burnout.

A 2013 Study on Burn-Out in the Workplace Found that:

85% of employees felt some stress in their job or career.

42 % of employees reported that job-related stress was negatively affecting one or more of their relationships.

35 % of employees said that pressure was threatening their physical or emotional well-being.

The following are the "**Top 5 Red Flags**" that burn-out is affecting you or your staff. Whether it's personal or professional burn-out, the symptoms remain the same.

"Weapons of Mass Instruction"

1. Mild or Advanced Frustration.

That usually causes unhealthy behavior at work such as bad tempers, grouchiness, and emotional outbursts, creating low productivity, low creativity, and bad relationships.

2. Chronic Exhaustion.

A persistent lack of energy that occurs when your employees lose their spirit. That leads to massive substandard performance and in some cases mild or horrific accidents. Fatigue and stress are the top two causes of workplace accidents in America.

3. Chronic Unhappiness.

The thought process here is, *"Everyday is bad."* That can also be a major symptom of depression. It can also accompany non-specific feelings that "something is wrong." Their attitude usually declines into a very negative space, and in some cases, you may notice an increase in drug and alcohol consumption.

4. Insecurity.

Insecurity is usually brought on as a result of distress and depression. In some cases this can be caused by increased drug and alcohol use, also creating feelings of alienation or isolation.

5. Health Issues.

That can include stress-related issues such as headaches, backaches, high blood pressure, insomnia and poor eyesight.

The five warning signs listed above can serve as red flags that you may be in--- or approaching burn-out. As I mentioned earlier, the faster burn-out is contained, the faster you can extinguish its flame.

"Weapons of Mass Instruction"

If your company has policies promoting proper rest, good nutrition, time-off, and adequate exercise such as walking, you can help workers fight burn-out.

Bouncing Back from Burn-Out:

1. **Take a Break** – During burn-out it's essential to slow down, take a long break and rest. Cut back on any unimportant activities and give your mind time to heal.
2. **Seek Out Support** – Reconnect with as many loved ones and friends as possible. Use them to express your feelings and release your emotions. That is what friends and family are for.
3. **Seek Out Professional Help** – This may be the most critical step of all. While family and friends are precious, sometimes a professional can help you to clarify your life, your priorities, and your goals. This mental adjustment can reward you with tremendous, life-long coping skills.

A Story

I was teaching in Buffalo, NY and a lovely lady from the class asked if she could speak to me in private about a personal matter. I agreed and met her during a break. She said she was suffering from severe burn-out and she blamed it on the physical and emotional side-effects of massive weight gain. She discussed her weight problem with me in detail. She has trouble breathing, problems walking, leg pains, and her husband is not attracted to her anymore. I asked her when the weight problem began and she said right after her baby was born. I politely and innocently told her that weight struggles were a common occurrence when new mothers give birth for the first time. In a dry tone, she responded, *"But I adopted my baby!"*

The Nugget – Sometimes the best way to discuss and confront your problems is with humor.

"Weapons of Mass Instruction"

Weapon # 13

Corporate Wellness and Meditation!

With several thousand medical articles published regarding the benefits of meditation, the mysterious cloud that once overshadowed the technique has faded. The only mystery surrounding meditation is why every single company and business in America is not yet teaching it to all of their employees. Apparently, they are not yet aware of its tremendous health benefits and how it can dramatically reduce health care costs. I know this weapon can help change that.

A good corporate wellness program will always include some instruction on meditation. The physical, emotional and psychological benefits of meditation can be accurately studied, measured and quantified. Meditation has been used successfully for stress management, controlling blood pressure, eliminating pain and headaches, heart patients, cancer care, AIDS treatments, insomnia, anxiety, stomach issues, and a myriad of other ailments plaguing people in the workplace. Recently, the United States Marines were successfully trained in the art of meditation as a tool to relax while improving focus and concentration.

There are many types of meditation, however, "active" and "passive" can provide the most benefit to the corporate world.

Passive Meditation is done it a quiet setting. Sitting with your eyes closed, you take several slow, deep breaths while relaxing your body and mind. The goal of passive meditation is to quiet your mind and eliminate distracting thoughts. While it's not like learning to play the piano, it does take a minimal amount of practice to help get the feel of it. However, the physical and mental health benefits are extraordinary!

Active Mediation is similar to passive except its goal is to keep the mind active while in this very peaceful state. The goal is (while at this deep level of relaxation), to keep the mind "thinking" because it is an excellent level for analyzing problems. Research shows that analyzing issues while in a meditative state causes your

"Weapons of Mass Instruction"

intuition to "turn on" or "kick in." At that point, with such an intense focus, you become aware of information to solve the problem which you were not aware of earlier due to stress or distractions. Also, active meditation carries with it the same health benefits as passive meditation.

Regardless of which type of meditation peaks your interest, it's critical that you start practicing. I would like to introduce you to a meditation technique I teach in my wellness seminars. It's effortless and easy to learn. It's a bit mechanical. However, I've noticed beginners appreciate the mechanical ritual because it makes it easier to apply. So here it goes:

Step 1 - Loosen any tight clothing, remove your glasses, turn off your cell phone, no gum in the mouth. Find a comfortable (sitting) position. Close your eyes. Take three gentle, very slow, deep breaths, and as you exhale merely let go and imagine you're relaxing.

Step 2 – Silently count backward slowly from 100-1, or 50-1, or 25-1, or the most popular 10-1.

Step 3 - Use your mind to slowly relax your body from your head all the way down to your toes, and imagine all tensions and ligament pressures in your body dissolving.

Step 4 - To help your mind to relax, simply visualize several tranquil and passive scenes. That puts your mind in neutral. Perhaps you're walking on the beach on a beautiful day. A day out fishing or a walk through the mountains may be a relaxing scene for you. Any scene that is passive will help you to relax mentally. If your mind wanders, this is natural. Do not worry about it; there's no right or wrong way to do this.

Step 5 - Once you're relaxed, just sit with your eyes closed for 5, 10 or 15 minutes, allowing your body to repair itself.

"Weapons of Mass Instruction"

Step 6 - When you desire to open your eyes, slowly count up from 1 to 5 and mentally tell yourself, *"I am wide awake, full of energy and feeling great!"*

It's ideal to practice this system once a day for 15 minutes. If you have time, practice two or even three times a day. The benefits will astound you. You should see an increase in your energy levels almost immediately. Several corporations I've worked with allow employees to take a 10-minute meditation break. They call it a "mind re-charge," and it improved productivity. Many clients I've worked with have also reported a healthy drop in their blood pressure. Others have reported headache and migraine relief. I've also taught the technique to children, and they learn it faster than adults. I consistently see their grades, memory, and concentration improve.

I'm sure this information has provided some motivation to adopt the practice of meditation into your lifestyle. Remember: "Everything in moderation except meditation."

Quote for Thought:

"There are powerful techniques such as meditation, which anyone can adopt." - Dalai Lama

"Weapons of Mass Instruction"

Weapon # 14

Corporate Wellness to Eliminate Habits!

A good corporate wellness program will include some training on behavior modification. When constructive habits multiply, you will notice very high productivity. When destructive habits increase, you will find your life and business rolling rapidly downhill.

Positive habits may include being polite, saving money, eating right, meditating, being loyal, performing high-quality work, time management, and the like.

Negative habits may include smoking, overeating, procrastination, drug abuse, gambling, alcohol abuse, cursing or nail-biting. While some harmful habits require professional therapy, others may be controlled by using your mind more effectively.

While teaching an advanced wellness program in New Jersey, I asked a volunteer from the audience to participate in a hypnosis demonstration. A student in the class named Bill quickly came forward. I asked Bill to have a seat, close his eyes and relax deeply.

After a series of deepening techniques, Bill was very relaxed and in deep hypnosis. While in hypnosis, I gave Bill a hypnotic suggestion to loosen and tighten his belt buckle every time I pointed my finger at him. Bill opened his eyes; then the fun began. While still standing in the front of the room, I started to ask Bill a series of unimportant, unrelated questions. Several times during this question and answer session I pointed my finger at Bill. Each time I pointed at him, he loosened or tightened his belt. Soon the class was laughing so loud that Bill wanted to know what was so funny.

I then let him in on the little secret. *"Bill, while you were in hypnosis, I programmed you to loosen and tighten your belt every time I pointed my finger at you."* At this time, I pointed my finger at Bill again, he began to reach for his belt,

"Weapons of Mass Instruction"

and suddenly he stopped halfway. Laughing hysterically, he said, *"Aha! I caught myself. Now that I know what you're doing, I choose not to cooperate."* The class and Bill truly enjoyed this demonstration; it also taught them the first step in habit control.

"You must first know that you have the habit and you must identify it. And you must have a strong desire to eliminate the habit."

The truth is people throughout the world eliminate destructive habits every day without any outside help. They do it without wellness programs, hypnosis, behavior modification, therapy, self-help CDs, or the like. The motivating force enabling them to succeed is a strong, powerful desire. If you wanted to stop smoking, you would have stopped. If you wanted to reduce weight, you would have already reduced it. If you wanted to stop spending money foolishly, you would stop. If you wanted to improve your work performance, you would have. If you wanted to improve a relationship, you would have.

"Desire is the ultimate motivational force behind all human behavior."

The moment that we understand the power of desire, we can begin to use its power to help us in the elimination or adaptation of certain habits for personal and professional success. We can use our new patterns to improve every area of our lives. Here are some great weapons to arm yourself with:

1. Identify the Habit You Wish to Eliminate.

Recognize that this habit is a crutch in your life that no longer needs to be there.

2. Strengthen Your Desire to Eliminate the Habit.

The stronger your desire, the faster your results. It is much easier to conquer a habit today than it will be tomorrow, so take action now. Begin by making a list of ten compelling reasons for eliminating the habit. Then, find ten more compelling reasons for each of the original ten. That is an excellent way to build your desire.

"Weapons of Mass Instruction"

Step 3 - Practice "Positive Habit Replacement."

That means that anytime you are about to engage in the harmful habit, *immediately stop what you are doing and perform a more positive activity.* For example, if you have the desire to smoke or overeat, stop what you are doing and instead take a walk, write a letter, brush your teeth, gargle, call a friend, read a book or drink a glass of water. These simple activities will begin to break the pattern --- the habit usually follows. As you continue to break the pattern in this manner, the negative habit will weaken and will eventually be replaced by the positive pattern.

Step 4 - Visualize Yourself Habit Free.

In your mind use all of your inner senses to assist in programming these new images into your nervous system. With your eyes closed, visualize and **see** yourself habit free. **Hear** others complimenting your new lifestyle. **Feel** the excitement rush through your body as you release the habit from your life. If applicable, **smell** and **taste** your success. Use your **inner voice** to describe how lucky you are, now that the pattern has been eliminated. Imagine a new and empowering habit replacing the old one.

Most of all, project yourself mentally several years into the future. From this future perspective, imagine yourself living free from the habit. Sense with all of your sincerity and emotion, all of the benefits you are enjoying with the new pattern firmly in place. In your mind, create a solid feeling of accomplishment and achievement.

Step 5 – Reward Yourself for Your Success.

As you successfully eliminate each habit, it's important to reward yourself. Perhaps you may buy yourself a small gift, have your nails done, treat yourself to a movie, or something similar.

Remember, every time you reward yourself for a specific success, you will dramatically build your desire to reach for higher ground with even greater success

"Weapons of Mass Instruction"

and productivity. These rewards serve as a reminder that you have accomplished something worthwhile and that you deserve the best that life has to offer.

"If you feel that your habit requires professional therapy, take action immediately. When you use these techniques in conjunction with a licensed professional, you will obtain faster results."

Let's Remember:

1. Identify the habit you wish to eliminate.
2. Strengthen your desire to remove the habit.
3. Find a positive habit to replace the old one.
4. Visualize yourself free from the habit.
5. Reward yourself.
6. Work with a healthcare professional if necessary.

Quote for Thought:

"A man who can't bear to share his habits is a man who needs to quit them." — *Stephen King, The Dark Tower*

"Weapons of Mass Instruction"

Weapon # 15

Help Your Employees to Stop Smoking!

Did you know that if you own a business and employ smokers, your bottom line is taking a direct hit that can sink a ship? That's right! Today, American companies are paying an estimated $3,391 extra, per smoker, per year in direct medical costs. That does not include a significant loss of productivity from smoking-related illnesses such as heart disease, stroke, cancer, and chronic respiratory diseases.

Approximately 425,000 Americans die every year due to smoking-related illnesses, so it's imperative to offer tips and programs to your employees to help them kick this nasty, suicidal habit.

I want you use this nugget as an aid to help your employees eliminate the smoking addiction permanently. Perhaps you can post it or reprint it in an accessible place for their future reference.

Based on research, I have assembled a significant **"9 Step Process"** designed to help the smoker kick the habit and minimize withdrawal. My success rate has been pretty incredible with this process, and I'm very proud of our accomplishments.

The research concludes that it's virtually impossible to stop smoking unless you are ready. You have to be willing to throw your cigarettes in the trash and take back control of your life. **You must be ready!** You have to let go of your failed excuses, and most of all stop fighting for your right to smoke. **Wake up! The war is over, and you've lost.**

Smokers have been cleverly deceived by an industry that calculatingly placed addictive substances into your cigarettes and made you a junkie. That's right; you're a junkie! The cigarette industry duped you, drugged you, took all your money, made you sick, and murdered you. These facts should raise enough anger within you that they motivate you to quit. Stop fighting for cigarettes and start fighting for you. Do this for yourself and your loved ones.

"Weapons of Mass Instruction"

Research also states that the most successful ex-smokers did not make it on their first try. It was on their 2nd or 3rd attempt that they succeeded. While it's important not to use this statistic as an excuse to fail, it's also important to remember to keep fighting until you win. Think back at all the time and effort you put into becoming a smoker. Don't you think it's worth it putting a little time and effort into breaking the addiction permanently? You certainly gave cigarettes a chance; now give your body and your life the same opportunity.

Here's what you need to know:

Once you put your cigarette out for the last time, it takes about seven days for nicotine to leave your body. For most people withdrawal is not a fun process, so the first seven days is usually the most difficult for some people. As I mentioned, the following **"9 Step Process,"** can be a great asset for making your withdrawal easier. As a result, your success rate will dramatically increase. All of these measures are easy to apply, while physiologically and psychologically--- they are sound. Remember, it's vital to utilize these steps for the next seven days as you pass nicotine.

9 Steps for the Next 7 Days!

Step 1 - Avoid Sugar.

This action can become very involved so here is the bite-sized version. Every time your sugar levels drop it triggers an urge to smoke. Avoiding sugar helps to keep your levels stable, therefore reducing the smoking urge while going through withdrawal. This step can also help you to prevent weight gain. However, fruits and fresh fruit juices are acceptable since these sugars are natural. It's important to remember to eat as much fruit and as many vegetables as possible for the next seven days.

"Weapons of Mass Instruction"

Step 2 - Have 3 Meals a Day Including Breakfast.

Three meals a day can help to keep your stomach full so that you won't crave junk foods. That can keep your weight down. Breakfast is critical for the next seven days, and you must include some proteins and complex carbohydrates. These tend to stabilize your sugar levels and substantially reduce smoking urges. Your breakfast can be as simple as toast, toast with peanut butter, low-fat cheese, low-fat milk, fruits, bananas, eggs, or a healthy cereal without sugar. It's recommended that you avoid any cereal that turns your milk into different colors.

Step 3 - Brush Your Teeth or Gargle after Every Meal.

Nicotine tends to remain in your saliva glands for about seven days. Therefore, after chewing and finishing a meal, that familiar taste will stay in your mouth triggering urges to smoke. The faster you clean your mouth after a meal, the less this will affect you. After seven days you never have to brush your teeth again. (HA!)

Step 4 - Buy a New Toothbrush.

It's essential that you start brushing your teeth with a new toothbrush. Because your old brush has been cleaning the filthy, dirty mouth of a smoker; it has nicotine on it. You end up swallowing the nicotine from your old brush; it goes directly into your bloodstream and triggers strong urges to smoke. Brushing with an old brush is a reason withdrawal takes much longer for some people, but--- not for you.

Step 5 - Drink 5 to 8 Glasses of Non-Caloric Liquids a Day.

Water, water with lemon, herbal teas, green teas, and seltzer help to flush nicotine out of your system making withdrawal faster and more bearable. If you keep a pitcher of water on your desk daily, this should be very easy.

"Weapons of Mass Instruction"

Step 6 - Increase Your Calcium Intake.

Milk, yogurt, cottage cheese, and leafy greens can be an excellent source of calcium. As nicotine is leaving your body, it takes your calcium with it. Calcium is an unusual mineral that helps us stay calm and relaxed. It's critical to remain calm and comfortable during the withdrawal period, so replacing your calcium can be an excellent tool to minimize withdrawal.

Step 7 - Take a B vitamin. (Preferably one with Biotin)

B vitamins have two nicknames; they are called "the emotional vitamin," or "stress tabs." While calcium is good for physical withdrawal, B vitamins help your mind. They can keep your emotions stable as your body passes nicotine. That is also very important in minimizing your withdrawal. For some people, a multivitamin is enough. However, most people need to take a full B. If your B has biotin in it, chances are it's a good B.

Step 8 - Avoid Alcohol & Caffeine for 7 Days.

Now before you get upset, this is a significant step, and it's only for seven days. The problem with alcohol is that it has sugar in it and that triggers the urge to smoke. Many people put large amounts of sugar in their coffee, and that can create the same issue described in step 1. The recommendation is to switch to decaf for a week. If you absolutely cannot avoid alcohol, be sure you do your drinking with a full belly of food. The food can help absorb the sugar from the drink and lessen your urges. Remember, many people associate cigarettes with coffee and alcohol, so be careful.

Step 9 - Quit with a Friend.

No question having a supportive friend (A.K.A. "Quit-Buddy") on your side is very beneficial. Should you get edgy, you can support each other, and also celebrate each other's victories. If you have a quit-buddy by your side, you

"Weapons of Mass Instruction"

dramatically increase your chances of remaining a non-smoker for the rest of your life.

"Please remember to consult with your health-care provider to be sure these suggestions are not in conflict with his/her recommendations."

Several years ago I was presenting this seminar at Lourdes Medical Center. One of the attendees was smoking seven and a half packs of cigarettes per day. (That's 150 cigarettes per day, or 54,750 a year.) He had open heart surgery and his left lung removed and still could not kick the habit. Four days after this program he stopped smoking and has been nicotine free for over four years.

I understand that quitting smoking is a tough decision to make and commit to. However, my goal is that these suggestions can help make your transition more comfortable, as you become a permanent, healthy non-smoker.

Let's Remember:

1. You must be ready to stop smoking.
2. Avoid sugar for the next seven days.
3. Have three meals a day including breakfast.
4. Brush your teeth after every meal.
5. Buy a new toothbrush.
6. Drink a lot of water.
7. Increase your calcium.
8. Take a B vitamin.
9. Avoid alcohol & caffeine for seven days.
10. Quit with a friend.

Quote for Thought:

"Cigarettes are killers that travel in packs" – Helen Francis

"Weapons of Mass Instruction"

Weapon # 16

Corporate Wellness and Walking!

Do you remember how much fun exercise was when we were children? We didn't call it exercise though; we called it jumping rope, kicking the can, skateboarding, playing hopscotch and running. When we grow up, we trade in all of our childhood activities for more important matters, such as busy schedules, overtime, lunch meetings and other serious responsibilities. Our days are too long, our free time is too sparse, and exercise becomes another chore to cram into our already hectic day.

I believe most of our population would rather have a severe case of hemorrhoids than to be subjected to exercise. To avoid the negative notion of exercise, people in the fitness field have substituted the word "movement" for the word "exercise," but most of us aren't fooled. It reminds me of used car dealerships changing the name of "used cars" to "pre-owned." It just sounds better. Regardless, it does not matter what you call it; exercise is exercise.

Today, more and more corporations and businesses are recommending that their employees integrate walking into their lifestyle. They even promote walking breaks during the workday. It simply is an excellent tool to manage stress, control anxiety, stay trim, raise your energy levels, and improve productivity.

In my quest for physical fitness, I joined a gym. However, my first gym experience was not a pleasant one as I was first introduced to a machine named "stair master" (which should be called a "modern human torture device"). At first, it looked rather harmless. I programmed its electronic pacer to level 17 (which I now know means *"pain"*), then I began walking and pumping. After only five minutes I could not believe how much I ached. My legs felt as if they would soon fall off, my heart was in my throat, and I had an Excedrin headache # 49. That didn't stop me though, I persisted and persisted. But by the third day, I couldn't take it anymore. I picked up what was left of my body, quit the gym and never went back. I'm not ashamed to say that I still have nightmares about it.

"Weapons of Mass Instruction"

My next logical step in my quest for fitness was jogging. I jogged for only three days, and then my ankles began to swell up like balloons and didn't normalize for two months. The pain was excruciating, and my doctor quickly put an end to my jogging career. From that point forward I disliked jogging, and I hated joggers (I used to chase them with my car). For many months after that, I would only exercise my thumb on the remote control of my television, and if I wanted an excellent cardiovascular workout, I would sit in the bathtub, take a bath, open the drain and fight the current. It was shortly after this I discovered the wonderful world of walking. Finally, an easy exercise that contained many health benefits and I could practice it without hurting myself. What a deal!

Walking is an excellent way to clear your mind, and it's the #1 vigorous aerobic exercise in our country for health and fitness. In a recent television interview, movie star Arnold Schwarzenegger said, *"In America, walking has now surpassed jogging."* This fact may be apparent once we understand how convenient walking can be. You do not need to visit a gym to walk. You can practice in your home, in a park, even in the mall, and the best part about walking is that it's FREE!

The health benefits of walking are numerous; this is a primary reason, so many corporations promote it to their employees. Larger organizations even have workout facilities. Some offer employees free memberships to local gyms and spas, due to the overwhelming savings on healthcare costs and the return on investment.

Check out these surprising facts:

*Walking helps to curb your appetite!

*Walking helps to prevent osteoporosis in women!

*Walking helps you to sleep better!

*Walking helps you to awaken with greater energy!

*Walking can help people with diabetes to use less insulin!

"Weapons of Mass Instruction"

*Walking helps to keep you slim and trim!

*Walking contributes to improving your sex life!

*Walking can help fade fibromyalgia pain!

*Walking helps prevent stroke risks!

*Walking helps to lift mild depression!

*Walking gives you an abundant amount of energy and flexibility!

*Walking is pleasantly addictive!

Although walking is a natural form of exercise, I recommend you consult your doctor or health care professional before attempting any exercise program. For best results, you should dress comfortably and wear loose clothing. Experts in the fitness field also advise wearing good walking shoes or sneakers.

If you come from "couch potato land," and you haven't exercised in years, start off slow. Before exercising, be sure that you warm up for at least five minutes to prevent injury and soreness. Warming up gently prepares the body for the upcoming walk or workout. Calisthenics or gentle stretching exercises are considered great warm-up activities. For maximum effectiveness, your walking routine should be practiced three to five times per week, at least thirty minutes each time. If you listen to music with earphones during your workout, time will indeed fly.

After your workout, you should also spend a few minutes "cooling down." Again, this provides your body with an adjustment period, and it helps to prevent soreness or injury. If you enjoy other types of exercise such as swimming, running, skipping rope, bench stepping, sports, bike riding, dancing, etc., you are giving your body an excellent gift. Always remember that your body is designed for movement and activity. You have approximately 640-850 muscles and over 200 bones within you,

"Weapons of Mass Instruction"

all begging to be kept active and young. The more you use your body, the stronger it will become. The stronger your body, the better it will serve you.

If your company does not yet have a wellness program that includes walking, perhaps it would be a good idea to mention it to someone with an open mind in human resources. You'll be doing yourself and your co-workers an excellent service.

Let's Remember:

1. Start off slow if you are a beginner.
2. Be sure you warm up and cool down.
3. Listen to music if possible.
4. Bring water with you if necessary, and a small cloth to wipe perspiration.
5. If possible, take the stairs instead of the elevator.

Quote for Thought:

"My grandmother started walking five miles a day when she was sixty. She's ninety-seven now, and we don't know where the heck she is." - *Ellen DeGeneres*

"Weapons of Mass Instruction"

Weapon # 17

Boost Your Productivity with Water!

How would you like to: enhance your productivity, lose weight, improve your health, eliminate fatigue, reduce headaches and improve your mood? It's all possible, and it's all FREE! The solution is drinking more water.

Several companies I've done training for have made water breaks a mandatory part of daily activity. Water is imperative for your energy and productivity. I recognize that most people acknowledge the importance of drinking water; I'm just concerned with how many of them consistently follow through. Do you drink enough water? Do you have a water cooler or fountain close to your work desk? Can you keep a pitcher of fresh water or bottled water at your workstation?

Approximately 70% of your body is made up of water. Your body needs water for basic survival. If you do not water your plants, they will die. Your body will also perish unless you water it daily. By drinking water and ingesting plenty of water-rich foods, you can create a slender, healthy body bursting with productive power. Did you know that water curbs the appetite, helping you to feel full? Water also improves your digestive and elimination processes giving your body more energy to tackle your day's activities.

How Much Water Should You Drink?

The Institute of Medicine sets general guidelines for total water intake. It recommends that women consume a total of 91 ounces (that's about 2.7 liters) per day – from all food and beverages combined. For men, it's approximately 125 ounces a day (or 3.7 liters). Depending on your diet, about 25% of the water you consume comes from your food.

"Weapons of Mass Instruction"

Are You Properly Hydrated?

A simple way to gauge your hydration levels is to look at your urine. It should be reasonably clear, however, if it is very dark yellow, that's a sign you may need to drink more water.

Dehydration has a direct link with cases of chronic fatigue. It's virtually impossible to be productive on the job if you're always tired. It can also be very dangerous if you work with heavy machinery. Water is used by your body as an aid to flush out toxins and waste products. When your body is low on water your heart needs to work harder pumping oxygenated blood to all your cells. That can create massive fatigue and is quite taxing on other bodily organs and functions.

Water helps your body to feel good, and this is one of the reasons your energy levels increase. Ultimately, when your body is operating in a peak state, it sends positive signals to your brain which dramatically affect your mood. An upward swing in your mood also has a direct impact on your productivity--- on the job or at home.

For your benefit, it is not recommended that you drink cold water or cold drinks while eating. Cold beverages **(while eating)** tend to freeze or hamper the digestive tract, causing improper digestion and zapping your energy levels. Consider switching to room temperature, cool, warm or hot beverages **while eating**. That is a step in the right direction.

There is also a "special secret" for transforming water from a "hydrator" to a "super-hydrator," giving your body even more significant benefits. What's the secret? Just add some lemon to your water. Lemon transforms basic water into a magical potion for health. It can:

*Reduce the amount of acid in your body.

*Keep your urinary tract clean and healthy.

*Aid in bodily detoxification.

"Weapons of Mass Instruction"

*Boost your immune system.

*Reduce phlegm production.

*Rejuvenate your skin.

*Reduce anxiety and depression.

*Provide greater mental clarity.

*All of which can enhance your productivity.

*This list can be endless.

My favorite beverage is Poland Spring Flavored Water. I promote it to all of my seminar participants and personally drink about two/six packs per day. It truly boosts my energy levels and is incredibly refreshing. No fat, no calories, no chemicals, no artificial flavoring, and they're sold in four great, natural flavors. However, Poland Spring is "real" sparkling flavored water. You must be aware of other brands that may contain chemicals and other unhealthy additives. Similarly, there are also beverages and additives that can act as natural dehydrators. You should be aware of these and use them in moderation.

The Top 5 Dehydrators:

1. Alcohol.

2. Caffeine.

3. Artificial Sweeteners.

4. Salt.

5. Cola Drinks.

"Weapons of Mass Instruction"

Finally, if you do not like to drink water, compromise and begin eating significant amounts of water-rich foods. Nutritionists recommend that your diet is made up of 70% water-rich foods. Start by eating lots of fresh fruits and vegetables. Iceberg lettuce, oranges, beets, watermelon and broccoli all have very high water content. They will help your body to cleanse and energize itself simultaneously. Follow these tips and weapons, and your productivity levels will go through the roof!

Let's Remember:

1. Ladies need about 91 ounces of water daily.
2. Men need about 125 ounces of water daily.
3. Water can boost your productivity through proper hydration.
4. Avoid icy cold drinks while eating.
5. Water with lemon is a powerful super-hydrator.

Quote for Thought:

"Water taken in moderation, cannot hurt anybody." – Mark Twain

"Weapons of Mass Instruction"

Weapon # 18

Stress Management in the Workplace!

An eighteen-year-old boy approached his ninety-nine-year-old grandmother for some advice on life. "Grandmother, you have lived such a long and healthy life, what are your secrets for such longevity," the grandson asked? The woman paused a moment in silent reflection, then replied, "I have no secrets, but I do have a word that I like to consider my motto." The grandson curiously asked, "What is that word, Grandmother?" "RELAX," she replied!

One of the most significant points to remember in this nugget is that stress is eating away at your bottom line and costing your company millions of dollars. More than 200 stress-related studies are detailed in scientific journals during the past three years. Stress has a significant link to every problem we face as a species. Stress causes us to snap under pressure; it breaks down positive communication in families and dramatically affects your work performance.

Stress also affects your mental health, your attitudes, and your personality. It's estimated that some 60 to 70% of all health problems are directly linked to stress since it appears to be a factor in more than two-thirds of visits to primary-care physicians. Stress deletes fifteen to twenty years from the human lifespan since it weakens the body's natural defenses by suppressing the immune system.

Stress taxes your nerves, muscles, and organs directly. Stress is linked to problems such as migraine and tension headaches, the common cold, ulcers, heart disease, strokes, stomach disorders, arthritic problems, allergies, multiple sclerosis and more.

Consider For a Moment the Following:

*At least one million Americans have a heart attack each year.

*Twelve million alcoholics in the United States find stress management in a bottle.

"Weapons of Mass Instruction"

*Americans consume tons of aspirin every day.

*Over eight million Americans have stomach disorders and ulcers.

*80% of Americans ingest some medical prescription each day, including thirteen billion tranquilizers, anti-depressants, barbiturates, diuretics, and amphetamines yearly.

*There are over fifty-thousand stress-related suicides each year in the United States.

Our Perceptions Give Birth to Stress!

"Psychologically, stress is an illusion created by the human mind."

Stress is not real. If stress were a real thing like gravity, it would affect everyone in the same way, but it does not. The fact is that the things that stress me out, should stress you out, but they don't. On the other hand, the things that stress you out should stress me out, but they don't. Why? Stressful events are created out of our perceptions, not from the event itself. All events are neutral until a human being internalizes and judges it.

The latest research indicates that stress and distress are *created by and in your mind.* That does not mean that the stressful event is not real; it just means that situations become stressful, according to how you subconsciously perceive the event as it unfolds. It's not the event or job that's stressing you out, but how you are internalizing it. How you internally perceive the stressor will determine if it will become a primary or minor one. How you internally represent outside events will determine whether its effect is harmful or beneficial. In other words, if you "think" the stressor is a major one, it will be major for you. If you "think" the stressor is minor, or a stepping stone to something better, that will be your reality. Simply put, "stress is in the eye of the beholder."

Let me give you an example. Imagine there are two office assistants with work piled very high on their desks. The first assistant is thinking, *"This is too much*

"Weapons of Mass Instruction"

work, I'll never get it done, I can't handle this pressure." While the second is thinking, *"This is a lot of work, but it will make the day go fast, and I won't be bored."* Assistant #1 is going to have a very stressful day and probably leave work with a headache or worse, just because he/she perceives her workload to be a *significant* stressor. If she continues to view the workload as overbearing, the stress may lead to physical and mental health problems.

Meanwhile, the second assistant has the same amount of work squeezed into the same time frame, yet he/she leaves work feeling great. Why? He perceives the heavy workload as creating a fast, productive day. Both had the same amount of work, but two completely different attitudes. Your perception is a powerful creator of any stressor.

If you're fired from your job, and you represent it to yourself as *"the end of the world,"* your stress levels will be very high. In contrast, if you believe the termination is the beginning of a brighter, more compelling career, your stress levels will not escalate. If while paying your bills you're thinking, *"I hate paying bills,"* your stress levels will be higher than the person who thinks, *"Thank God I can afford to pay these bills."* If you cry, *"Don't leave me, I'm nothing without you,"* as your lover walks out on you, your stress levels will be higher than the person who thinks, *"Hallelujah, now I can find someone deserving of me!"*

The primary difference in these examples is what took place in the individual's head, the individual's perception, **not the event itself.** Therefore, our attitude plays a significant role in helping us to triumph over stress. When stress motivates us to take action and stimulates creativity, it's okay. When pressure creates overwhelming anxieties, it's time for an attitude adjustment.

From the many available books on stress and the varied techniques they offer, I have chosen the three strategies that have been the *most* beneficial for me. Each will make substantial changes in the quality of your life. I have been using the following for many years with very satisfactory results, all of which are further discussed in this book.

"Weapons of Mass Instruction"

* **Meditation** (For physical & mental relaxation.)

* **Exercise** (For keeping your body in shape and tension relief.)

* **Maintenance of a positive attitude** (For managing your day to day hassles.)

Stress management techniques are easy, but like anything worthwhile, they must be applied. The more you practice, the greater the benefits you will receive personally and professionally. Sometimes people do not care about their health until they lose it. That is also true with top executives.

Here are ten other tips that can help you beat personal and professional stress. Check with your healthcare provider and make sure these suggestions are in harmony with his or her recommendations. Begin using these preventive techniques today so that you will have a healthier tomorrow.

1. Practice meditation (Page 52) and easy exercise (Page 64) daily.

2. Do not eat unless you are hungry. Using food to combat stress will only result in unnecessary weight gain and other issues.

3. Some research indicates that playing with a pet or participating in a favorite hobby can have many beneficial effects.

4. Smile often, cultivate your sense of humor and laugh as much as possible. Read comic strips daily, watch cartoons, see funny movies, and laugh at yourself.

5. Listen to soothing music when possible; it helps to quiet your mind.

6. Excess sugar can heighten your stress response, so limit your sugar intake by reading package labels.

7. Take a B vitamin to control your emotions (preferably one that contains biotin).

8. Eat lots of fiber, starches, and carbohydrates since these tend to have a calming effect on the body. Always eat breakfast.

"Weapons of Mass Instruction"

9. Leave your job at the office; do not take it home with you. You do not get paid to think about your job on <u>your</u> time. Schedule some play and vacation time.

10. Learn and master the art of asking yourself positive questions. In each stressful situation silently ask yourself:

A. *"What can I learn from this situation?"*

B. *"How can I deal with this constructively?"*

C. *"What's funny about this?"*

D. *"What can I do to prevent this from happening again?"*

E. *"Does this event contain any benefits?"*

By asking yourself positive questions while in stressful situations, your mind can help you to perceive negative situations in a favorable light. Positive questions allow your mind to seek out solutions you may not be able to recognize due to the stressful influence. This simple attitude shift can make a significant difference in how you view certain situations, and how you deal with stress.

Quote for Thought:

"There cannot be a stressful crisis next week; my schedule is already full." – *Henry Kissinger*

"Weapons of Mass Instruction"

Weapon # 19

Dealing with Temper Tantrums in the Office!

Imagine an office place where everyone behaved in a calm, rational, and adult manner. Wow, what a concept! Unfortunately, some people never completely grow up regardless of their position in the company. From the mail room all the way up to the CEO in some cases, many people have adult bodies, but the mentality of a two-year-old.

Like two-year-olds, individuals who throw temper tantrums believe they are entitled to get their way. This group often includes immature high-level executives who think that having power gives them the right to treat others any way they like. They feel free to abuse anyone who gets in their way.

However, the simple truth is that adult temper tantrums are a learned behavior. By the age of two, the young child has learned that he or she can get anything they want, exactly when they want it, by crying and screaming. The sad truth is that the child carried this immature behavior into adulthood - and it still works. It always gets them what they want because the adults at the opposite end of this childish onslaught keep letting them get away with it. We never confront them or tell them, "No!" As a result, the behavior reinforces itself as an "infantile mechanism" for getting your way. It's juvenile, immature, silly and very sad. What a crime that some people never grow up. They also have no clue as to what others are thinking about them.

If you have to deal with immature bosses, co-workers, employees, or team members, I'm sure the four suggestions below will help you keep your sanity.

1. The Best Response Is No Response.

Stay quiet and calm until the person is relaxed and ready to have a civilized conversation. Let them rant and rave without interruption until they run out of steam and deflate. Never interrupt them or argue back. Never ask them to calm down or change their feelings. All of this will backfire on you. You can pass the time by watching their behavior in amazement and try to be entertained by it. If you try hard, you'll find that their infantile displays can be very amusing.

2. Never Show Fear, Anger or any other Emotional Reaction.

Those responses will be gratifying to the individual throwing a tantrum. Always remember that people act in specific ways because they were taught there is some payoff for their behavior. When someone acts this childish, you must be the adult. Your anger and fear can add fuel to the tantrum, and at the same time, you are teaching them that they have control over you. You have shown them that the best way to get an emotional response from you is for them to have a "hissy fit." You have taught them how to push your buttons. For your safety, peace of mind, and mental health; it is critical that you never reveal your buttons to anyone-EVER! That can be your downfall since corporate America has so many people who enjoy pushing other people's buttons.

3. Maintain Your Confidence and Composure.

These are the qualities of an exceptional leader. Use relaxed body language, soft eye contact, and a gentle, respectful tone of voice to reduce the "emotional temperature" of the cry-baby adult. Explain that tantrums are inappropriate at work, and they are detrimental to the team. Human resources must explain that if the outbursts continue---they will be fired. Don't worry about being too harsh; merely be direct, professional, and relaxed. Remember, you are speaking to a child in an adult body. Your respectful, gentle tone is for the child, and your directness is for the adult.

4. Do Not Avoid Each Other.

Although it's tempting to avoid each other after a negative outburst or conflict; my research shows that it's better to try and keep the peace by treating each other with respect. That is central in human relations skills.

"Weapons of Mass Instruction"

If you are a manager or supervisor who is not known for emotional outbursts, then teach your team to strive for open, honest conversations and problem-solving. Train your team to acknowledge situations resulting in disagreements without an angry exchange. If this does not help, then give the whining co-worker a rattle, a bib, and a bottle.

Let's Remember:

1. The best response to a tantrum is no response at all.
2. Never display any emotional responses.
3. Maintain your composure and confidence levels.
4. Don't avoid each other.
5. Treat each other with respect.

Quote for Thought:

"It's my rule never to lose my temper till it would be detrimental to keep it." - Sean O'Casey

"Weapons of Mass Instruction"

Weapon # 20

Tips to Remain Calm During an Argument!

1. Do you get involved in a lot of arguments?
2. Are most of your arguments of a gentle nature, or are they loud and obnoxious?
3. Has an argument ever cost you a relationship or job?

The average person has about 5000 arguments in a lifetime; if you're married, that statistic could double. At least half of our arguments revolve around insignificant nonsense. However, the rest can quickly transform into full-blown battles if you don't have the skills to remain calm, cool, and collected during the squabble.

With an employment termination rate of 29% associated with the inability to get along with others, and a divorce rate much higher than that, we need to master strategies to prevent arguments from escalating. You need to learn strategies for keeping your head on straight when negative people cross your path. The ability to do this with poise and grace is what separates us from the animal kingdom. In challenging encounters, the default of an animal is to instantaneously "react" then "attack." The human default is to first "think," then to "respond." Many of us have forgotten that the ability to "choose to respond" rather than "react without thought" is an alternative still readily available to us.

In our country incidents like road rage or fighting for a parking space have resulted in unnecessary suffering and death because people can't control their tempers. We need to learn to choose strategies and behaviors that may not necessarily help us win an argument, but instead help us to re-channel the angry energy, creating something more positive and constructive. It is in "reacting" that we destroy and in "responding" that we rebuild.

With that in mind, let's arm ourselves with some powerful weapons to diffuse or circumvent the argumentative process so that even in the most highly charged situations you can maintain your composure and professionalism.

"Weapons of Mass Instruction"

1. Remain Detached from their Personality.

Truthfully, in a heated argument, this can be difficult for you to do, especially if you have an ego the size of Texas. However, this is the only strategy standing between you and the possibility of a full-blown escalation. In a heated debate, the more you focus on their personality, the more things you'll find wrong with them. You'll also become more emotionally attached. That will cause you to judge them more unsympathetically, dislike them tremendously, and eventually, your anger meter will explode all over your freshly painted walls.

2. Focus Only on the Solution or Goal.

That is a master strategy used by professionals who seem to avoid or circumvent arguments consistently. By choosing to keep your laser-sharp focus **only on the solution or goal,** your mind and emotions tend to become solution-oriented, rather than looking for justice or revenge. The justice is served when the problem is resolved, not if it exacerbates. That is the thought process of a master.

3. Practice Deep Breathing.

Many people are not aware of the fact that in stressful situations we don't breathe properly. That usually causes our stress and emotional levels to intensify. That is the main reason all stress management techniques involve the act of deep breathing. It sounds so over simplistic, but it's imperative. Breathing helps your body to calm down naturally. Breathing oxygenates your brain and body, allowing you to maintain control and think clearly.

"It is with clear thoughts that we act wisely."

Take caution, however, that your deep breathing does not resemble someone who is getting ready to rumble and throw the first punch. Your breathing should be deep, peaceful, and controlled.

"Weapons of Mass Instruction"

4. Avoid Sarcasm, Ridicule, and Mockery.

Sarcasm, ridicule, and mockery are definite signs that you're focusing on their personality. These are the words of a person who wants to hurt another, rather than heal. Negative, sarcastic remarks only throw fuel on the fire. It's best to remain calm and quiet while waiting for your turn to speak.

5. Try to Understand the Other Person's Viewpoint.

Hidden beneath the foundation of every argument is the fact that many people just want to be heard and understood. Understanding the other person's point of view will swiftly squash many disagreements. I've been in situations where the argument was not worth my precious time, and I gracefully conceded to the other party. Sometimes you have to ask yourself, *"Do I want to be happy or right?"* That is a compelling question that will put you in a position to give yourself a good reality check.

6. Take a Break if the Pressure is Getting to You.

That is an excellent way to disconnect from the situation and get centered. Go to the bathroom, wash your face, get some water, take some more deep breaths, remember something funny, or think of a loved one. As you begin to feel your power return, then jump back into the ring.

Naturally, none of these strategies are going to help you to live a life free of arguments, and that's not the goal. The actual goal is to recognize that an argument can be a tool for understanding and appreciating another person's point of view, whether or not we agree with it. No matter how significant or insignificant the squabble was, there's always room to learn something from another human being. Just remember it's easier to learn if you remain calm and composed.

"Weapons of Mass Instruction"

A Parable

After eating an entire bull, the lion fell to the ground and roared with pleasure. The lion roared long and loud enough to attract a hunter. The hunter cautiously approached the loud roaring lion and shot it dead.

The Nugget - When you're full of bull, keep your mouth shut.

Let's Remember:

1. Remain detached from their personality.
2. Focus only on the solution or outcome.
3. Practice deep breathing.
4. Avoid being sarcastic.
5. Try to see the issue from their perspective.
6. Take a time-out if things get heated.
7. People just want to be heard and understood.
8. It is with clear thoughts that we act wisely.
9. Give yourself a reality check.

Quote for Thought:

"The other night I ate at a real nice family restaurant, and every table had an argument going." – George Carlin

"Weapons of Mass Instruction"

Weapon # 21

Dealing with Crying in the Workplace!

Crying is a natural, normal response to a highly charged emotional situation. The situation could be a negative one or a very happy one. Crying creates a strong emotional release in the human body, and it's excellent for stress management. In fact, a recent medical article stated that 85% of women interviewed claimed that they felt better and were more relaxed after a good cry. However, it seems that the opposite is also true; holding in your tears and holding back your emotions appears to have a weakening effect on the immune system.

It seems that crying is becoming more acceptable, even for men. America's speaker of the house, John Boehner has been known to break down publicly many times. His persistent public crying has earned him the nickname, "weeper of the house."

Despite the fact that crying is a typical response to stimuli, we must remember there is still a time and place for everything. Therefore, tears in the workplace can be as awkward as having a laughing fit at a funeral.

My experience in the field has also taught me that tears can be used as a tool to manipulate and take advantage of others. For those of you who are familiar with my work, you know I'm a firm believer in the adage, *"what you allow, you teach."*

If you allow someone to continually physically or verbally abuse you, you are teaching them that it's OK. If you consistently let someone to walk all over you, you are showing them it's OK. The same can be said for crying in the workplace. If you allow an employee have their way or break company culture because they cried; you're teaching them that tears are a strategy for influencing your decision-making. You've shown them where you're weak and where your buttons are, and you can be sure they'll use the same tactic again for future manipulation.

"Weapons of Mass Instruction"

Now, while we don't want to assume that all tears are for manipulative purposes automatically; we do want to protect ourselves from such a scheme and at the same time be genuinely empathetic.

Here are four simple steps and weapons you can utilize to correct the problem empathetically.

Step 1 - Take the Crier off the Floor into a Private Room.

In this manner, you can save them further embarrassment, and help them get better control of themselves. In some cases, the privacy may cause them to lose even greater control, but this should be OK. Remember, the release of emotions is a healthy way to let off steam. Depending on the situation, you may want to bring an additional person into the room as a witness and for support.

Step 2 - Hand them a Tissue.

The tissue allows them to dry themselves but also sends two powerful subconscious messages: First: that you are empathetic to their situation and are there to assist in any way you can. Second: that tears in the office will only get you a tissue---nothing else!

Step 3 - Talk them Through It.

That is an important step and must be done empathetically, never sympathetically. An empathetic approach on your part will help you to keep the situation more stable and much more professional. A sympathetic approach means you are getting emotionally involved with the issue and drawn into it. An empathetic approach allows you to remain professionally neutral.

"With empathy, you are putting yourself in their shoes to better relate, with sympathy you are taking ownership of their shoes."

Listen to their issues carefully, and when it's your turn to speak, use an even, calm, conversational tone.

"Weapons of Mass Instruction"

Step 4 - Consider a Time Out.

If the above steps are unsuccessful because the crying is so out of control, this may be an excellent opportunity to give the person a break to be alone. That will offer them a moment to calm down and to compose themselves. The break should only be about 15 minutes. If you provide them with a more extended amount of time, you are teaching them that tears can get them some time off. A professional time-out statement might sound like this: *"(Name), to help you relax; I'll give you a 15-minute break and some breathing room."* After 15 minutes, continue your intervention.

People skills are essential in the workplace. I don't know how a business can survive without them. I'm very confident if you need the above tools they will help you out of some tight spots.

Let's Remember:

1. Take the crier off the floor quickly.
2. Hand them a tissue.
3. Talk them through it.
4. Consider a time-out. (Only if necessary.)

Quote for Thought:

"When someone is crying, of course, the noble thing to do is to comfort them. But if someone is trying to hide their tears, it may also be noble to pretend you do not notice them." - Lemony Snicket, *Horseradish: Bitter Truths You Can't Avoid*

"Weapons of Mass Instruction"

Weapon # 22

Please, Help! My Boss Is Hitting on Me!

I had the joy of speaking with a lady in a recent seminar who posed a question and used the following words: *"Mr. Jacobsen, can you please give me advice? My supervisor has started to hit on me by dropping subtle hints that he's interested. I have no interest in him at all! He has body odor, saliva balls caked in the corners of his mouth, and always has food caught between his teeth. What should I do?"* After I stopped laughing, I gave her these common sense tips.

If a man is into you, he will take any innocent signal you send and transform it into a permission slip for a date. It could be the way you dress, your smile, your perfume, or even a particular look you give. I'm not saying that the way you dress and your perfume is causing the problem; it's not your fault. I'm saying men misread cues and vibes. To protect yourself, be sure you are not sending mixed messages.

However, if a supervisor or co-worker is "always" hitting on you, the responsibility will eventually fall back on you. You have not been direct enough with them, or you're doing something unconsciously that's sending out the wrong vibe. If you are straightforward enough with a man the first time, they usually get the hint and retreat quickly. If you delay your directness, you are setting yourself up for more issues or harassment. If you have no interest in the individual, you must LET THEM KNOW IMMEDIATELY. Simple, direct, and polite refusals will usually do the trick. For example:

"No thank you, I have no interest in dating people I work with."

"No thank you, I'm seeing someone else."

"No thank you, I only desire to keep our relationship professional."

"No thank you, I'm busy the rest of my life taking care of my 17 children."

"Weapons of Mass Instruction"

If they respond with something like, "I understand; how about just going out for some coffee?" That is a clear indication that you have not been direct enough. Since you are in a professional setting and dealing with your boss, you must make sure that your body language, your tone of voice and your words are congruently saying "NO!" Again, be sure you are not sending mixed messages.

Though it may sound obvious, it's also essential you avoid situations where you're alone with your boss. This type of situation can also send a signal that you're interested. Try to mingle only in a group setting. That is the best way to avoid an uncomfortable situation.

Finally, if your direct, honest approach has not tamed the beast, you may need to take it up with human resources and check with your company's sexual harassment policies. I'm sure you don't want anything as simple as an offer to go out on a date to turn into a lengthy litigation.

Let's Remember:

1. It's easy for people to misread signals.
2. Be polite and direct at your first refusal.
3. Be sure your words, tone of voice and body language are congruent.
4. Avoid situations where you are alone with this person.
5. Educate yourself on the sexual harassment rules of your company.

Quote for Thought:

"Dating on the job can be a blessing or a curse." – John Gray

"Weapons of Mass Instruction"

Weapon # 23

The 6 Qualities of a Healthy Personality!

Would you like to advance your professional and personal image? Would you like people to remember you by your confidence, flair, style, and most of all by your spirit? Your personality and how you project it is the ultimate key to achieving these goals.

Your personality is the development of organized patterns, behaviors, and attitudes that make you distinct. Combined, they create a healthy, attractive persona causing you to stand out and be remembered. In the corporate and public sectors, a pleasing personality can climb the success ladder much quicker than someone with a nasty or gloomy disposition. The employee with the personality of a dial tone rarely gets anywhere near the ladder.

There are six distinct traits or qualities that people with healthy personalities possess. If you take a moment to reflect on some of our planet's most successful and memorable people, you will notice that they all possessed these six traits in one form or another. Even if your personality doesn't shine like a highly polished diamond, you'll be amazed at how much progress you can make in a very short time. These traits are not reserved for only select people. The good news is everyone can develop a healthy personality with minimal time and practice. Let's take a look at the six qualities to get a better understanding of how easy it really can be.

Quality # 1 - They Rarely Complain!

Logically, there is a time and place for complaining. However, chronic complainers are chronic downers, and most people do not want to associate with them. It requires no musical talent to harp on something constantly. When necessary, healthy personalities complain in a "professional manner." That means: they wait for the opportune moment, they rarely raise their voices, they are never derogatory, they never point fingers, and most of all they focus on solutions with

"Weapons of Mass Instruction"

"win-win" outcomes. If more people were trained to be "solution-oriented" rather than "problem-centered," complaining would become extinct.

Quality # 2 - They Easily Forgive!

It's very rare for a healthy personality to hold grudges. That's because they have a healthy self-esteem which helps them not to take things personally. Although you cannot use them as doormats, it's very rare that a healthy personality is plotting revenge or seeking to destroy anyone in any way. For the sake of your physiological and psychological health, always be mindful that it is far better to forgive and forget than to hate and remember.

Quality # 3 - They Get Along with <u>Lots</u> of <u>Different</u> Types of People!

Notice: They don't only get along with lots of people—they get along with lots of "different" types of people. That is an incredible skill that more people need to possess. Regardless of color, race, belief system, or sexual orientation, the healthy personality has excellent rapport skills and can find common ground with any person. They usually build strong bonds with co-workers and friends, and this quality affords them healthy, long-term relationships.

Quality # 4 - They Maintain a Positive Mental Attitude! – (PMA)

Positive thinking will not help you do anything, but positive thinking can help you do **everything** better than negative thinking. Therefore, a positive mental attitude at home and on the job is a critical component to your success. No one has ever suffered a severe case of eye strain by looking on the bright side of things, and this is what the healthy personality does so well. While they acknowledge or recognize negativity, they keep their eyes focused or fixed on the positive. Employees with a PMA climb the ladder of success faster than toxic, jaundiced, negative people.

Quality # 5 - They Are Assertive!

Assertiveness is another critical component to a healthy personality. Assertive behavior respects the needs and interests of all people. Instead of arrogance, they project a healthy sense of pride. Instead of greed, their focus is on achievement. Rather than competition, they think "win-win." A healthy personality is a natural result or byproduct of assertiveness.

Quality # 6 - They Smile & Laugh A Lot!

The American Medical Association states that smiling & laughing creates many positive, healthy effects in your body. Laughing reduces your stress and helps to enhance immune functioning. A recent research report suggests that people with a highly developed sense of humor are less prone to illness. Did you know your smile can be a predictor of how long you'll live -- and that a simple smile has a measurable effect on your overall well-being? Smiling can help alleviate emotional pain and has a powerful impact on your mood. At the same time, your smile can change the attitude of others. The average preschooler laughs about 450 times per day; while the average adult laughs about 15 times per day. A person with a healthy personality smiles approximately 150-200 times per day. That could be the main reason why so many people gravitate towards them. Remember, the direction of your day always goes in the direction that the corners of your mouth point. Therefore, laughter and smiling is the best medicine for soul-ache and should be taken in large doses. Perhaps we should all go back to preschool.

Let's Remember:

1. They rarely complain.
2. They easily forgive.
3. They get along with lots of different types of people.
4. Positive mental attitude.
5. They are assertive.
6. They smile and laugh a lot.

Quote for Thought:

"It's easy to spot the person with a great personality----they always remind you so much of yourself." Danny Kaye

"Weapons of Mass Instruction"

Weapon # 24

Dealing with Negative People!

How many of you work with at least one negative, toxic, low-life, jaundiced, downbeat, depressing, venomous, jaded, cynical person? How many of you drive into work, and as soon as you see their car you get pissed? Negative people, also known as "Negensteins," (combination of negative + Frankenstein) can be real downers. There's one in every family, every business, and every team. You can place one negenstein on a team of 25 people, and their attitude can quickly destroy the team morale. They always see the dark side of things, they regularly use negative terminology, and they have the personality of a wet mop.

Are there any strategies for effectively working with these types of characters? Are there any coping techniques to apply if you live with or are married to a negenstein? There's an old expression about "walking a mile in someone's shoes," and I believe this can help us understand why negensteins act the way they do. Truthfully, once we know someone's internal programming, it's easier for us to have some mercy on them.

For our purposes, negativity is defined as *"out of control pessimism."* There are two types of negativity: "Situational" and "Chronic."

Situational negativity is a realistic, healthy, natural response to any unexpected or fearful circumstance. This type of negativity is quite healthy because it serves to protect you by keeping you on your toes. Once the negative event passes, most people release the negativity and go on with their lives.

Chronic negativity is similar to situational, except in this case negenstein's hold on to the negativity, dwell on it, and never let it go. They live it, breathe it, and talk about it. They also enjoy company, so they are continually looking for recruits.

Negative thinking is a learned behavior. We learn negative patterns at a very early age by modeling our parents, television stars, our friends, and our teachers. All

"Weapons of Mass Instruction"

underachievers maintain a negative attitude. Their negativity allows them to lead a mediocre life without guilt. Negative thinking serves as an internal coping mechanism which protects them from disappointment and fear. Their negative ideology acts as a "protective mechanism." When failure, discontentment or misfortune happens in the life of a negenstein, their negative attitude can ease the blow--- and even justify it.

By shedding negativity on others, it helps them feel less lonely and gives them a false sense of power and control. In other words, all negative behaviors are utilized for some subconscious "pay off."

"These negative behaviors are mal-adaptive defenses of the ego."

These defenses worked in their younger, formative years where they were learned, but are no longer appropriate as an adult.

As an example, I'm sure you work with at least one **"Expert-Know it all."** They know everything about everything, (at least they think they do). This personality type can be a challenge to work with. However, as with all negative behavior, it's used as a protective mechanism and cry for help. The "know it all" is utilizing that false front to cover up insecurity. By acting smarter than they are, they hope that you won't realize that--- they are not. Their "payoff" is the belief that they won't be "found out." Actually, a "real expert" has something to say, while the "know it all," just wants to say something. In reality, a real, genuine expert never has to tell you that they are.

When you accurately analyze the "know-it-all" behavior, it can be kind of sad. While that doesn't excuse their behavior, it should remind you that they need to be treated objectively as someone you should take caution with.

Another favorite negenstein is the **"Control-Freak."** You may know one of these, and as with all negensteins, this is another personality born out of fear. They deliberately control situations that *they already know they can handle* to reinforce their power to themselves and others. In this case, their payoff is the safety in not

"Weapons of Mass Instruction"

being found out that they feel powerless. While that doesn't excuse their behavior, it should remind you that they need to be treated objectively as someone you must deal with cautiously.

What about the **"Chronic Complainer?"** This negenstein cries, whines, and moans all day long about everything. Their favorite pastime is giving co-workers headaches. You may have heard the expression, "squeaky wheel gets the grease." The expression of the chronic complainer is, "squeaky wheel gets the---gifts!" The gifts they so desperately desire are *"attention"* and *"to be heard."* This negenstein believes that no one likes them, and complaining is their tool for getting noticed. In other words, they'd rather have negative attention than no attention at all. While that doesn't excuse their behavior, it should remind you that they need to be treated objectively as someone you must deal with cautiously.

"The Gossip" in your office is suffering from a sad case of loneliness. That is why they generously spread the latest news and rumors around the office. Therefore, gossip is a tool used to get attention and to feel superior. The idea is that I know something you don't, and I have the power to decide whether or not to tell you. They also use gossip as a "here's my gift to you" approach if they're trying to get you to like them. Again, while that doesn't excuse their behavior, it should remind you that they need to be treated objectively as someone you must deal with cautiously.

The most dangerous of all negensteins is **"The Back-Stabber,"** because unlike the others, they deliberately hurt people. Unlike the others, the back-stabber is also a real coward because they intentionally hurt you when you're not looking or not around. These people are so unhappy with themselves and their life situation that they have no emotional resources. They use back-stabbing as a tool to get control and to feel falsely empowered. As sad as that sounds, therein lies your revenge. You must take that power away from them. Therefore, the most efficient way to deal with a back-stabber is an immediate confrontation. The longer you wait to confront them the more damage they can do. A direct confrontation tells them that you have no fear and that they can't hurt you. The moment a back-stabber realizes

"Weapons of Mass Instruction"

they can't harm you, they'll retreat and leave you alone, realizing they won't get any empowerment from you.

There are plenty of informational resources available that can teach you every strategy you need to know about dealing with negative people. However, I would like to give the whole scene a different twist. I have three steps that I've successfully applied to negative situations and negative people that I'd like to share with you now. At least 1 of the three steps has helped me in every negative encounter. These actions or weapons may be different from what you're used to, but work with them and let me know about your successes.

1. Ignore it!

As over simplistic as that sounds, if you are in a position where ignoring the negenstein benefits you, then take that route. You don't have to fight every battle that comes your way. Again, you don't have to fight every battle that comes your way. If you can't ignore it then, apply the next two steps.

2. Protect Yourself from them.

If you can't ignore them, then you must protect yourself. That is done by not allowing negensteins to learn that they have affected you in any way. Even if you have to fake it, never let them know that they got to you. They look for people's buttons and weaknesses. They are always searching for a path into your head, and by exposing your buttons, they will be happy to push them. If you don't want anyone to get your goat, don't let them know where it's tied up. If they already know where your goat is---then MOVE IT!

3. Try to Help them.

This one is my favorite, and I've been successful with it many times. I confidently and politely confront the person about the issue or situation and ask them if there's any way I can help. If they tell me to go to hell, I go back and apply step 1. If they

"Weapons of Mass Instruction"

seem gracious and welcome the assistance, I'll go out of my way to try and make it better.

Despite the fact that negensteins reveal themselves in different personality styles; there is one other interesting fact that they all have in common.

"Negative people do not know that they're negative. Negative people think they're positive."

That fact now leads us to you. Is it possible you're a negenstein and don't realize it? That is very common, and you may need to do a reality check on yourself. Sometimes we're so busy minding other people's negativity that we let ours get out of hand.

Is it possible people are talking behind your back? Can it be when people see you coming they hide behind a corner? Suppose you're the one in the office who is perceived as being negative?

There are three steps you can apply that will help you bounce back and recover.

1. Ask Your Most Trusted Friends for Feedback.

Just ask, *"Do you think I'm negative in any way?"* If they respond that you do have negenstein tendencies, it's essential that you *do not kill the messenger.* Don't get upset, or angry with them, and most of all don't defend yourself. You asked them for help, and they graciously gave you the answer. The best response is to listen carefully, take it all in, and then politely thank them.

2. Continuously Monitor Yourself.

Develop a checklist based on information gathered from your friends and track yourself. Continue to ask your friends for feedback or progress status, and reward yourself as you slowly make the required positive changes.

"Weapons of Mass Instruction"

3. Always Look for Opportunities to be Positive and Optimistic.

Find positive things to say and do, even if at first you have to overdo it a little. Read positive and uplifting books to shift your moods. Most of all stop hanging out with negensteins, by changing your friends or associates if need be.

Dealing with negative and challenging people is an intense subject. However, in the corporate world, the optimistic people climb the ladder of success much faster than the negative people. They also remain in their jobs for a more extended period. My observations have been, the more you monitor yourself, and the more you avoid the downside of things, you'll remain on the optimistic highway for years to come.

Let's Remember:

1. Negativity is out of control pessimism.
2. Situational negativity is usually healthy and natural.
3. Chronic negativity is an unrealistic response to external events.
4. Negativity is a learned behavior.
5. All negative behavior is rewarded with a subconscious payoff.
6. Negative reactions are mal-adaptive defenses of the ego.
7. You don't have to fight every battle that comes your way.

Quote for Thought:

"There's only one negative person in the world, but he travels a lot." – Zig Ziglar

"Weapons of Mass Instruction"

Weapon # 25

The Magic of Conflict

If you're looking for a unique way to improve your team's communication skills, or to enhance a relationship, or increase your group's productivity; why not try creating a conflict? Believe me; it will help! Were you aware that every significant achievement since the beginning of time was born out of the ashes of a conflict? It's true! Conflict has been a significant resource and ally for anyone desiring change. The words "conflict" & "change" are synonymous.

While I'm not asking you to create a conflict calculatingly; I am asking you to view your clashes in a different light. With the right attitude and appropriate communication skills, your conflicts will become a powerful tool for creating positive change and growth. This rule also applies to your family and business life.

Conflict is inevitable because of human differences. That is especially true in the business world where all of your problems come on two legs and can talk back.

I'd like to introduce you to a progressive conflict resolution strategy that I've seen produce some robust results. I call it, **"The 5 Steps to Cooperative Resolution."** While these steps are common sense, I've noticed that in many highly charged conflicts, common sense is not all that common. People know the rules, yet anger and frustration can cause us to forget our manners and trigger a conflict escalation.

The 1st Step in Conflict Resolution is Preventing the Conflict from Escalating.

That is done most efficiently by confronting the problem, person, or situation immediately. Never wait! The moment a conflict exposes its ugly face---confront! My experience has consistently shown me that most conflicts become overwhelming because they were not nipped in the bud. The longer you wait to confront, the more intense and problematic your conflict will grow. In many cases, this will damage relationships.

"Weapons of Mass Instruction"

The 2nd Step is to Set Up a Meeting in a Neutral Locale Where Together, You Can Brainstorm Solutions.

It's ideal to meet in a place away from where the problem originated. Negative emotions from the surrounding environment may cause the person to put up their guard making troubleshooting more difficult. A favorite tactic is to conduct your problem-solving session outside of the office or in a restaurant while having breakfast, lunch or dinner.

The 3rd Step is the Actual Brainstorming Session.

Brainstorming solutions must be approached with care. Remember your goal is not only to resolve, but to preserve the relationship. Here, your people skills are essential.

Be sure to meet and greet the other party with an optimistic statement. That is the most positive way to begin a resolution process. Several good opening remarks may be:

"I'm glad we can get together and resolve this issue."

"I'm sure we can agree swiftly."

"Thank you for your determination in bringing this issue to an end."

Make sure you use "I" statements and speak in an even, conversational tone. That will help to build trust and create a lot of rapport, essential for problem-solving. Also, avoid bringing up the past and instead focus only on the topic at hand. These ideas will also help the other party feel more comfortable and maintain their composure.

Most of all continually focus on areas that you have in common. Finding common ground in a resolution process allows you to see solutions you may have overlooked.

"Weapons of Mass Instruction"

The 4th Step is Requesting Behavioral Changes Only.

As a unique problem-solving note: Never ask people to "feel differently," or "be different," or to "change their attitude." These are requests that you do not have the right to ask of any human being. Remember, you are only allowed to request "behavioral changes." The actual magic of conflict lies not in trying to change others, but to use conflict as a stepping stone toward greater working relationships and more efficient resolution skills.

The 5th Step is to Put the Agreement in Writing.

When you arrive at an agreeable solution, you must then get the agreement in writing. You may spend hours, days, or weeks in the resolution process yet if the agreement is not in writing all of your time was wasted. Remember, if it's not in writing, it never happened. Although a written agreement may not be appropriate in the family arena, it's still important for everyone to agree to the new terms.

Let's Remember:

1. The ideal situation is to prevent the conflict from escalating.
2. Set up a neutral location for the resolution session.
3. Brainstorm various solutions and remain open to all possibilities.
4. Put the agreement in writing.
5. Only request behavioral changes.

Quote for Thought:

"Conflict is not seeing eye to eye, but mouth to mouth." – Og Mandino

"Weapons of Mass Instruction"

Weapon # 26

A New Concept - Win, Win, Heal!

Conflict is inevitable because of human differences. I'd like to take a moment now and explain the various outcomes you can expect during a resolution process. Depending on your problem-solving abilities or skills, experts in the field tell us you can expect 1 of 5 outcomes during a problem-solving process. The purpose of this nugget or weapon is to offer you a "possible 6th outcome" that most people never discuss or teach. However, I believe it's the most important and valuable of all. I've already casually mentioned it several times.

There Are 3 Types of Conflicts:

1. Unilateral

2. Bi-lateral

3. Joint

Over 65% of all conflicts are *unilateral or personal problems,* meaning you can resolve them on your own without involving any outside help. A *bilateral* conflict usually involves two people or parties, and both are required for the resolution to transpire. The third is a *joint* conflict, and that typically involves small or large groups of people or teams. In many cases, joint conflicts require 3rd party resolution experts, facilitators, and mediators. With the right tools and common sense, 90% of conflicts can be resolved. Unfortunately, with the right tools and common sense, some conflicts cannot be resolved. That is because some people thrive on spreading negativity and conflict.

"Weapons of Mass Instruction"

There Are Usually 2 Reasons for Bilateral or Joint Conflicts:

1. We Have *Different* Interests.

For example:

    A. I want to go out to dinner, and you want to stay home.
    B. I want to move to Florida, and you prefer California.
    C. I want to be on your team, and you are not interested in working with me.
    D. I want to resolve an issue, and you can't be bothered.

2. We Have the *Same* Interests, Which Are in Conflict.

For example:

    A. We're both applying for the same job position.
    B. Some new office space just became available, and we both want it.
    C. We both want the same week off for vacation, and it's not realistic for the company.
    D. I want to sell my car, and you want to buy it. My asking price is $10,000, and you only want to pay $7500.

When resolving conflict with the tools and strategies discussed in the last chapter, the problem can usually have any 1 of 5 outcomes:

1. Win-Lose.

In this scenario, I win, and you lose. This outcome is beneficial for me and unfortunate for you. I walk away from the negotiation table smiling, and you walk away harboring bitterness and resentment. This result leaves the problem unresolved in your mind and chances are extremely high that I have not heard the last of you. This issue will quickly rise again, and we'll both be back at the negotiation table soon.

"Weapons of Mass Instruction"

2. Lose-Win.

In this scenario, I lose, and you win. This outcome is beneficial for you and unfortunate for me. You walk away from the negotiation table smiling, and I walk away harboring bitterness and resentment. This result leaves the problem unresolved in my mind and chances are extremely high that you have not heard the last of me. This issue will quickly rise again, and we'll both be back at the negotiation table soon.

3. Lose-Lose.

Here is a familiar scenario, especially for those with weak communication, problem-solving, and negotiation skills. It's also popular for people who lose their tempers quickly or don't know what they want. Interestingly, for negensteins, this outcome is considered an opportunity for revenge. Their warped thought process is that *"I may have lost, but at least I took you with me."*

4. Compromise.

To compromise is to make a deal between different parties where each party gives up part of their demand. In this outcome, all parties win and lose simultaneously. In other words, they each get a little of what they want--- and don't want. A compromise is a standard resolution tactic found in politics.

5. Win-Win.

Win-Win is a term made famous by Steven Covey in his fantastic book, "The 7 Habits of Highly Effective People." Win-Win is sometimes misunderstood and must be defined in the following two ways:

A. Win-Win means everyone concerned has all of their demands or requests met to the fullest extent. In other words, everyone gets what they want, and they live happily ever after.

"Weapons of Mass Instruction"

B. Win-Win does not necessarily mean you'll get everything you want, and all of your demands met. It does mean that all parties concerned get so much of what they wanted, and even some extra unexpected bonuses, that everyone walks away from the table satisfied with no underlying bitterness.

Therein lies a critical distinction, so let's review it.

*"A Win-Win does not necessarily mean you will have all of your demands met. However, all parties concerned get so much of what they wanted, and even some extra unexpected perks and benefits, that everyone walks away from the table satisfied with no underlying bitterness. If there is ever any underlying bitterness, resentment, or hostility, it is **not** considered a Win-Win. Instead, it is a compromise."*

Creating a Win-Win outcome during a resolution process requires a unique set of common denominators. These five denominators must be brought to the decision table before problem-solving begins:

1. Both parties are very sincere and committed to resolving the issue.

2. Both sides have a strong desire for mutual gain. (Let's both win!)

3. Both sides are excellent communicators.

4. Both parties know exactly what they want.

5. Both parties have good negotiation skills.

I mentioned earlier; there is a 6th outcome that I enjoy sharing in my seminars. All of my participants appreciate the insight, and it's always very well received. It's an outcome not readily discussed in conflict resolution strategies, but I find it an enlightened route for those who are seeking real value in their problem-solving abilities. I call it:

"Weapons of Mass Instruction"

6. Win-Win-Heal!

Win-Win-Heal is very similar to a Win-Win. Actually, a Win-Win-Heal will have the identical outcomes as a standard Win-Win. The massive distinction lies in the fact that after the Win-Win is achieved, the relationship between both parties is completely healed, repaired and in a better place. This mindset is an enlightened way to resolve problems because its focus is entirely based on **mutual gain** and **relationship enrichment**. This type of worldview completely surpasses the people who only rush to the table to see what they can get without any regard for the other parties interests.

Perhaps one day our political, national, and global measuring stick for determining your problem-solving skills will not be judged by how many resolutions you've achieved, but instead by how many relationships you've restored along the way.

A Story

I know a man who spent the remaining years of his life planning an act of revenge for his greatest adversary. They could never find the tools or courage to bury the hatchet and remain friends. He spent years and sleepless nights trying to formulate his foe's demise. The years of stress and hateful planning must have been too much for the man. He died before he could release his vengeance.

The Nugget - Forgive your enemies - if you can't get back at them any other way.

"Weapons of Mass Instruction"

Weapon # 27

When's the Best Time to Avoid Conflict?

If you work at a job or career where other people are involved, conflict is unavoidable. The fastest way to reduce your apprehension towards conflict is to accept it as an inescapable part of your life and our world. An important fact worth repeating is that conflict is inevitable because of human differences.

Research from the Virginia Department of Human Resource Management states that "60 to 80 percent of all workplace conflict stems from strained or tense relationships between employees and executives." More proof that when people are involved conflict is usually not far behind.

Although most of us would rather avoid or circumvent conflict any time it raises its ugly head; it may not always be a good idea because of the significant positive benefits an adequately resolved conflict can create.

If you have the proper communication tools, people skills, negotiating skills, and problem-solving strategies; conflict can be a blessing. Adequately resolved conflict creates unity of purpose, heals relationships, improves communication, and more importantly leads directly to successful future collaborations. Indeed, if the dispute is handled correctly, it can also lead to better decision-making and enhanced creativity.

Regardless, for many people avoiding conflict is often the easiest way to deal with it. However, the process of "avoiding" does not make the conflict disappear but instead pushes it under the surface for a while until it reappears in a more monstrous form.

Irrespective of the benefits conflict resolution can bring, research concludes that there are four specific conflict situations worth avoiding if it is within your power. Regardless of your conflict resolution skill level, becoming entangled with these four types of conflict will usually create a "lose-lose" outcome.

"Weapons of Mass Instruction"

1. Avoid Conflicts About Rules & Regulations.

At this point, most people would ask, *"If I avoid conflicts revolving around rules and regulations, how can I change outdated policies, procedures, and processes?"* That's a great question! While I am a firm believer that a single person acting alone can change the world; statistically speaking, this type of conflict is easier to resolve if it involves a group effort rather than one sole person. If you alone possess the proper communication tools, people skills, negotiating skills, and problem-solving strategies—go for it. If not, this is a good conflict to avoid unless you have a team behind you.

2. Avoid Conflicts Threatening Your Job or Security.

I would think that this one was a no-brainer, but apparently, it is not. If someone puts a gun to your head and demands your money, it's not the time to whip out your conflict resolution guidebook to decide your next move. It's also not a good opportunity to try out your bargaining and negotiation skills. One of my favorite expressions is to, *"Choose your battles wisely."* This particular conflict situation may be a perfect time to intelligently weigh your pros and cons, and keep that expression in mind.

3. Avoid Conflicts Challenging Core Beliefs or Values.

Unless your favorite pastime is sharpening your argumentative skills, this is a great conflict to avoid. I'm sure you have more important personal and professional conflicts in which you can polish your skills. People's psychological makeup is a construction of their beliefs and values. Their ideas and values create who they are. By asking people to alter their values, you're asking them to modify their individuality and their internal wiring completely. That is a great conflict to avoid because of the difficulty involved in getting people to see out of their box. However, if you have time to waste—go for it!

"Weapons of Mass Instruction"

4. Avoid Conflicts Where the Other Party Does Not Want to Resolve.

This situation is the most difficult of all to cope with and the most difficult to accept. It can be tough if it encompasses a family relationship. However, the fact is that some people do not want to resolve or "play nice." Some people need time to cool down, and some people get stuck in their viewpoint and can't think or see out of that box. That is a good conflict to avoid because you may be spinning your wheels and wasting valuable time on a person or issue that may not be worth it. As a last resort, this is the perfect conflict situation where a mediator may prove to be particularly valuable. Often a good mediator can also coach employees through an existing conflict, helping them to build skills for handling future difficulties.

Let's Remember:

1. Avoid conflicts regarding rules & regulations.
2. Avoid conflicts where your security or job is threatened.
3. Avoid conflicts where core beliefs or values are challenged.
4. Avoid conflicts where the other party has no interest in resolving.

Quote for Thought:

"If you pick the wrong fight and win, you still lose."- General Herbert Norman Schwarzkopf, Jr.

"Weapons of Mass Instruction"

Weapon # 28

When to Walk Away from a Conflict….And not Look Back!

A Parable

A monkey shoved his hand and arm into a long-necked bottle to grab some peanuts that were lying on the bottom. When his hand was full, he ran into a small dilemma. His tightly closed fist packed with peanuts was now too large to retrieve from the bottle's thin neck. His hand and arm fit neatly in and out of the bottle while his hand was empty, but the moment he made a fist - he was stuck.

The Nugget - Sometimes we have to learn to let go.

What happens when you've applied every strategy, technique and resolution tactic and nothing helps? What happens when you invest hours or years in a resolution process only to end up in a position that's worse than where you started? When is the best time to just walk away, let go and not look back?

That is an awkward position to be in because walking away is the absolute last resort when everything else has failed. You may have to permanently say goodbye to a career, a job, or a relationship. Here is a critical point to remember:

"When you decide to walk, your timing must be perfect, or you may suffer some personal or professional setbacks."

For example, some people walk away **"too early"** and regret not giving it one more chance, or trying a different resolution approach. Walking away too soon can also deprive you of the resolution skills and lessons you could have developed by sticking around or working harder. Remember, every conflict you resolve helps to perfect your resolution skills.

Some people in battered relationships wait around and leave **"too late."** In many cases, they end up emotionally and physically maltreated and scarred. On the other

"Weapons of Mass Instruction"

hand, some people **"never walk away"** and live a life of inner and outer turmoil with a complete sense of hopelessness.

Walking away may be the best option after you have used all your power to resolve a conflict without positive results, Research into human problem solving concludes that if you can answer "YES" to any one of the following three questions, you are in a perfect position to let go and walk away. Your timing will be in alignment with your values. Therefore regrets or guilt can be minimal. If you can answer "Yes" to all 3--- perhaps you should have already walked a long time ago.

Question # 1 - Am I putting in more than I'm getting out?

That is an excellent and insightful question simply because if you're exerting tremendous energy without reaping any benefits, the chances are that same pattern will continue long into your future. If you find yourself answering "Yes" to this question, you must ask yourself, *"Is this a price I'm willing to pay?"* In this particular situation, your "cost" may far outweigh the "price."

Question # 2 - Is the conflict damaging the relationship and others?

Walking away and letting go may prove to be an excellent solution if the conflict is causing relationship damage. In this case, the question to ask yourself is, *"Am I willing to lose or permanently damage this relationship so I can win?"* Another issue is, *"Can I live happily in this situation if the conflict is left unresolved?"* If your answer is "Yes," focus on the more positive aspects of the relationship and drop the conflict.

Question # 3 - Is the conflict damaging me?

That is the most critical question of all. How is this conflict destroying you personally? Is your health at stake? Is your sanity impaired? Is your safety threatened in any way? Will remaining in this career, job, or relationship, create irreparable damage in your life? If the answer is "Yes," walk away and let go quickly.

"Weapons of Mass Instruction"

Walking away requires what I call, **"The 3 Shifts."** You must shift your mind, your heart, and your body.

1. You **shift your mind** and attitude to a place that realizes you've done everything in your power to no avail.
2. You **shift your heart** by sincerely forgiving yourself and the party involved.
3. Finally, **you shift your body** by turning it towards the door, confidently moving your legs in a forward motion, and preventing your head from ever turning back.

I'd like to close with a thought-provoking parable that neatly sums up the weapons discussed; it's called, "The Bear who wouldn't Stop Crying."

"The Bear who wouldn't Stop Crying."

While walking in a zoo, a man noticed a large bear hysterically crying, sobbing, and moaning. *"Why is that large brown bear crying,"* the man curiously asked the zookeeper? *"Because that bear is sitting on a large rusty nail,"* responded the zookeeper. More puzzled the man asked, *"Why doesn't the bear get off the nail if it hurts so much?"* The zookeeper looked at the man and said, *"The nail hurts just enough to make him cry, but not enough to make him move."*

The Nugget - Do not wait until things are so bad, or hurt so much, that you are forced to change. Make necessary changes now. Don't wait until it hurts enough.

Let's Remember:

1. The goal is to walk away at the right time.
2. Am I putting in more than I'm getting out?
3. Is the conflict damaging the relationship?
4. If the relationship is worth more than the conflict, focus on the more positive aspects of the relationship and drop the conflict.
5. Is the conflict damaging me?

"Weapons of Mass Instruction"

Quote for Thought:

"Most people would rather look backward than forward because it's easier to remember where you've been than to figure out where you're going." – Les Brown

"Weapons of Mass Instruction"

Weapon # 29

The 8 Primary Communication Bloopers!

Have you ever been involved in a conversation that seemed to flow effortlessly as you and your party seamlessly exchanged information? On the other hand, have you ever participated in the same type of exchange and felt like you were beating a dead horse? The conversation seemed to be hitting a brick wall while you and your party had no rapport?

These terrible communication traps happen all too often, especially in the business community. It seems that while we get caught up in our hectic, fast-paced day, the rules of effective communication get lost or forgotten. An essential rule I follow and share with others is the importance of regularly reviewing and practicing "the basics." That is a key to communication mastery.

My research into the communication field demonstrates that there are eight cardinal bloopers made in many communications. These eight bloopers can cause problem-solving to falter, relationships to crumble, hurt feelings, and violate rapport. Let's review all 8, and as a rule of thumb, try to keep them "sacred" as we interact with others on a personal and professional level. My goal in this weapon is to enhance your communication abilities and at the same time boost your professional and personal interactions.

1. Not Listening.

Notice that this blooper is listed at number one. It is a widespread error for your mind to wander occasionally, and for you to lose track of what someone was saying. For this mistake, you politely apologize and move on. Deliberately not paying attention will cause a massive problem in your relationships. The primary goal of a communication process is to exchange information and at the same time build stronger relationships. That can't be accomplished if you don't listen. If your goal is to climb the corporate ladder, make the big sale, mediate conflict, or build

"Weapons of Mass Instruction"

better relationships with your family---become a better listener. (We'll discuss this further in weapon # 30.)

2. Chronic Interrupting.

This blooper is quickly resolved by just re-learning our manners. It's not polite to interrupt others while they are speaking. It demonstrates that you are a poor listener with a damaged self-esteem. It shows your lack of concern for the person talking, and also sends a signal to others that you are rude. This mistake will cause you to lose credibility quickly! Credibility is essential in customer service and sales.

3. Criticism in Public.

That is one of the fastest ways to annihilate your credibility, destroy your integrity, violate rapport, and lose friends. Please remember what I'm about to say now because it's crucial: *"Even if you think you are God Almighty, you have no right, nor the authority to criticize any human being in public."* Anyone who has had any basic training in people skills understands that all criticism MUST be spoken in private. Criticism must also be carried out with a goal to build the individual's self-esteem, while at the same time correcting behavior. Therefore, during a critique process, keep your focus on the behavior or situation, never the person or their personality traits. (We'll discuss this further in weapons # 33 and # 34.)

4. Sarcasm & Ridicule.

Whereas criticism is usually aimed at a personal behavior; sarcasm and ridicule is often a negative remark made directly about the person. It is always rude and used to create some mockery, harm or hurt feelings. If your communication goal is to generate interconnectedness, rapport and build self-esteem, then avoid sarcasm & ridicule at all costs - especially in public.

"Weapons of Mass Instruction"

5. Talking Down or Above Someone.

Like sarcasm, ridicule, and criticism; this is another cardinal communication problem. It sends a message to the listener that you are smarter or more intelligent than they are. It conveys that you are above them in every way, while at the same time it--- hurts feelings. The most important thing to remember is that talking down also conveys the message that your self-esteem is severely damaged. There are two ways to have the tallest building in the city: First - build the tallest building, or second - knock everyone else's building down. How do you want to be remembered --- as a builder or a destroyer?

6. Pompous Word Usage.

These are large words used in a conversation that you know the listener will not understand. These include all types of jargon, slang, lingo and "50 cent words used in a 5 cent conversation." Pompous word usage is one of the fastest ways to turn a listener off since it creates an awkward separation between you and your listener. There are two types of people who use pompous words: First, is the person who is so highly educated, they know of no other way to express themselves. (We can forgive these folks.) Second, is the person who is only trying to impress you. Factually, pompous words just make you appear to be an arrogant person. Remember, it is extremely obfuscating to promulgate any complex or lengthy lexicon. (HA!)

7. Gossip of Any Kind.

I was brought up to never talk about anyone behind their back. Never say anything about anyone that you would not say to their face. Most of all, when you gossip about others, you are not defining them, you are describing yourself as someone who needs to gossip. And everyone who has witnessed your gossip now knows you are "that" type of person. Avoiding gossip defines your character and advances your professional image.

"Weapons of Mass Instruction"

8. Making Yourself More Important than the Listener.

This final communication blooper neatly sums up or encapsulates the last seven. You are well on your way to rock-solid communication skills and healthy relationships if you approach everyone as if they are your equal. The fact is - they are!

I mentioned earlier that the most important rule I follow is the importance of continually reviewing and practicing "the basics." Doing the "opposite" of these 8 are the basics. It's proper and polite conversation at its finest. Remember to keep them "sacred" as we interact with others on a personal and professional level.

Let's Remember:

1. Be a good listener.
2. Speak when it's your turn.
3. Avoid criticism in public.
4. Avoid sarcasm and ridicule.
5. Speak to people at their level.
6. Use easy to understand terminology.
7. Speak kindly of others.
8. See everyone as your equal.

Quote for Thought:

"Communication is listening twice as much as talking." - Bert Decker

"Weapons of Mass Instruction"

Weapon # 30

Listening with Both Ears!

A horse walks into a bar, and the bartender asks, "Hey, why the long face?"

I heard the great comedian; Frank Gorshin tell that joke in 1995. Hopefully, you remember him; his most famous acting role was as the Riddler in the Batman live-action television series of the 1960s. Perhaps the joke isn't that funny, but it does contain a lesson if you're listening with both ears.

Why would someone ask a horse such a stupid question? Isn't the bartender educated enough to realize that all horses have the same long face and head? Is it possible the bartender flunked out of his hippology classes? Was the bartender so drunk that he didn't realize that he was talking to a horse? Was the lighting in the bar so dim that he couldn't see that he was talking to a horse? I apologize for dissecting such a simple joke so unmercifully. However, all of that probing did eventually lead me to a satisfying answer which will become the focus of this weapon. The lesson here is the only people who would ask a horse about their long face are the people who are just not paying attention. Therein lies the first secret of being a good listener; **you have to pay attention to the person speaking to you.**

"The definition of listening is to give your full attention."

Unfortunately, instead of listening, most people are trying to think about what they're going to say next. This rude act turns your listening devices off, causing you to go into an internal daydream state. Many people drift so deep that they don't even realize the other person has stopped talking, usually followed by that awkward moment of dead, embarrassing silence. Many opportunities are missed because we are broadcasting when we should be listening. Remember, there are two kinds of bores---those who talk too much and those who listen too little. Which one are you?

"Weapons of Mass Instruction"

There are several simple strategies that you can employ to focus yourself when you're required to listen and give your complete attention.

1. Body Language.

STOP whatever you're doing to listen and hear. Turn your full body towards the person you are listening to and try to lean in slightly towards them as if what they're saying is the most exciting information you've ever heard. While you never want to invade anyone's space, this is a useful tool to cue your mind to focus.

2. Eye Contact.

Look directly into the person's **eyes** and at their **face** while they are talking; just be sure it does not turn into a stalking or awkward staring contest. There's nothing worse than someone staring into your eyes as if they're trying to put a spell on you. Looking directly at someone's face is more acceptable and less threatening than staring them down with constant eye contact. Eye and face contact are great tools because they allow you to observe the person's facial features as they are delivering their message. Watching someone's face and eyes also enable you to view and hear what the person is not verbally saying; that is an essential strategy for listening with both ears. Always remember that people say more with their body language than they do with their mouth. 93% of all communication is non-verbal.

3. Repeat their Words in Your Mind.

Here is another powerful, but simple tool. As the person talks, occasionally repeat the words they are speaking in your mind as if in playback mode. That is another fantastic signal to your mind to remain focused, and it also improves your recall of the conversation or information.

4. Don't Judge!

Another critical key for listening with both ears is not to judge the information as the speaker is transmitting it to you. Judgment turns your listening devices off,

"Weapons of Mass Instruction"

causing you to take another internal daydream trip to the land of criticism and assessment. As long as you're judging and pre-judging the incoming information, you may hear it, but you are not listening to it. Remember, hearing takes one ear, listening takes two.

5. Give Verbal and Non-Verbal Responses.

That is significant! You must let the listener know that you're alive and that all the lights are on in your brain. There is nothing worse than speaking to someone who has the "deer in headlight look" on their face. Smile, or nod your head, or lean in closer, or say, *"OK,"* or *"Uh-Huh."* Just remember never to interrupt until they are finished. Take a tip from nature---your ears aren't made to close, but your mouth is! Remember, a closed mouth gathers no feet.

Listed below, I have several listening questions. Take a brief moment and honestly answer each. If they help you notice a weakness, begin to focus on that area and correct it. In your business and personal life, listening or focusing your attention with both ears is a skill that cannot be neglected.

QUESTIONS:

1. Do you let people finish what they're trying to say before you speak?
2. Do you stop what you're doing and give 100% of your attention?
3. Do you give the person appropriate verbals & non-verbals as they speak?
4. Do you always listen with an open mind?
5. Do you begin rudely texting as a person is speaking?
6. Do you curb your own opinions, emotions, or judgments as they speak?
7. Do you talk about "nothing" to just fill in the silence?
8. Do you observe the person's body language as they speak?
9. Do you ask intelligent questions to clarify meaning?
10. Do you repeat their words in your mind?

"Weapons of Mass Instruction"

I had a funny conversation with my dad recently. It was funnier than the joke about the horse. The best part is that it reinforces some of what we've just discussed. I've written the conversation out in script format to convey the humor better.

ME – Hi, Dad! How are you?

DAD – Not good, not good, things are terrible and very bad!

ME - Why, what's wrong?

DAD – Well, you know how your mom tells those long, boring stories right in the middle of the baseball game, and I pretend that I'm listening?

ME – Yes.

DAD – Well, now after she tells the long, boring story, she asks me to repeat back everything she just said.

Let's Remember:

1. When someone is speaking to you, immediately STOP what you are doing and turn your full body towards them.
2. Practice proper face & eye contact.
3. Never stalk anyone with your eyes.
4. Repeat their words in your mind.
5. Don't judge!
6. Give verbal and nonverbal acknowledgments.

Quote for Thought:

"The golden rule of friendship is to listen to others as you would have them listen to you." – Gandhi

"Weapons of Mass Instruction"

Weapon # 31

Characteristics of a Great Leader!

For many years now I've been a fan and practitioner of "NLP or "Neuro-Linguistic Programming." NLP is the study of how we communicate with ourselves and others on an internal and external level. NLP teaches a potent strategy called, "Modeling," which is a very extensive subject. The principle of modeling is the replication and transfer of human capabilities from one person to another. That means by imitating the behaviors and abilities of someone successful in a chosen field; you can create the same successful outcomes, or better. Babies use the same method when learning to communicate; they utilize a trial and error approach by mimicking or modeling the people around them.

That is one of the reasons I enjoy working with and studying different people. I love to learn what makes people tick and their various strategies for success and development. I like modeling and emulating people who have gone where I have not yet been. Due to different life experiences, every human being has learned and developed their patterns and roads to success. These patterns are similar to recipes which when applied can duplicate the same results. Modeling offers us insights and strategies on how to observe and elicit the success patterns of other people. Once mastered, modeling can be an extraordinary life tool.

So, if modeling successful people is a valid tool, what are the success patterns or common traits found in great leaders? If you want to be a leader you need to know what makes them tick, how they think, and how they behave. John Quincy Adams was the sixth President of the United States (1825–1829). He served as an American diplomat, Senator, and Congressional representative. JQA once said, *"If your actions inspire others to dream more, learn more and do more, you are a leader."*

Does that mean that I don't need to be a Commanding General, a President, a King, a Queen, a Prime Minister, or a CEO of a massive company to be considered

"Weapons of Mass Instruction"

a great leader? That's correct! Most of our world's most significant leaders go unnoticed except by those who know them. I'm talking about the parents working two or more jobs to support their families, the teachers who work overtime to aid students needing extra care, the doctors or nurses who hold a patient's hand in a time of hopelessness, or the person volunteering their time in a soup kitchen feeding the hungry.

These people are great leaders because they lead people to better lives, and they help those who cannot help themselves. Though they are not celebrities, famous, or recognized on a global scale, that type of status is not essential to them. Like all great leaders, they acquire their acclaim by meticulously getting the job done and by serving others. The fact is all excellent leaders large or small are all made up of the same stuff. They intrinsically have six unique traits or qualities that separate them from other people. The most exciting part about this information is that once you are aware of these qualities, you can model these behaviors for yourself, and duplicate the results in your business or personal life. Great leaders are not made overnight. However, the following insights into their persona can make your journey a little easier and much more insightful.

1. Unmatched Passion & Energy.

Their abundant energy is a by-product of their immense passion for what they do and who they serve. Passion is an overwhelming zest, excitement, and zeal for a lifestyle, a completion of a goal, or the journey towards a vision. Leaders have no problems jumping out of bed in the morning eager to begin their day.

2. Impeccable Character.

Their character is a detailed list of unique features that define who they are, and it separates them from others. That list includes humility, assertiveness, high self-esteem, courage, decency, and the instinctive ability to connect with other people.

"Weapons of Mass Instruction"

3. High Levels of Integrity.

Defined as a steadfast adherence to a strict moral or ethical code; their code revolves around honesty and achievement while focusing on self and others. In a mock mathematical formula, Character + Integrity = Honor. Can you think of any "real" leader that is not worthy of honor?

4. Strong Desire to Serve.

Their strong desire to serve their code, their values, and most of all other people, is an essential component when modeling leaders. Think of some of the "real" leaders who have lived in our lifetime, and recognize the tremendous contributions they've made to our civilization and people worldwide. A false leader is interested in the fleece; a real leader is engaged with the flock.

5. Great Vision.

Eyesight is what you see when your eyes are open; vision is what you see when your eyes are closed. Leaders can create a vision in their mind and then transform that idea into a reality; this is a sign of genuine power. They have creative insights before others do. They see what others do not, which is critical in times of calamity when there is no known path. Today, many businesses and corporations are praised for their "ideas." However, a leader is a visionary who can take those ideas from the conceptual, and mold them into something concrete and viable. Whether it's leading your family or leading a country, without a vision people will perish.

6. Creates Leaders.

A "real" leader is not judged by how many followers they have, but instead by how many followers they transform into leaders. I know you've heard the expression, *"Give someone a fish and they eat for a day. Teach someone to fish, and they eat for a lifetime."* Leaders don't lead to gather apostles or side-kicks. Leaders create people who no longer need leaders. Show me any great leader, and I'll show you a more significant leader who led that great leader first.

"Weapons of Mass Instruction"

Let's Remember:

1. Unmatched passion and energy.
2. Impeccable character.
3. The highest level of integrity.
4. A strong desire to serve.
5. A true visionary.
6. Creates more leaders.

Quote for Thought:

"The business of a leader is to turn a weakness into strength, obstacles into stepping stones, and disaster into triumph." – Herbert Hoover

"Weapons of Mass Instruction"

Weapon # 32

3 Power Steps for Becoming More Assertive!

While I dislike the fine-art of labeling people, I do find this topic to be quite significant. At a closer look it may not be labeling people at all, but instead marking people's behavioral style and how it affects their life and success.

The three behavior styles I'd like to address and focus on are - The Passive, The Aggressive, and the Assertive. While each style is unique and has distinct characteristics, every human being has each style alive within themselves. The style that you demonstrate or is the most dominant in your personality usually fluctuates according to the situation or occasion. That is quite normal.

A severe personality issue arises, however, if a person favors one style without the ability to shift to the others when required. If you are locked into one dominant style without the flexibility to utilize the others at a moment's notice, it can dramatically affect your dealings with people on a broad scale. Let's take a look at all three styles:

The Passive – This is sometimes the dominant pattern of someone with a severely damaged self-esteem. They have a nickname, "D.O.O.R.M.A.T.S," which is an acronym for, "The Dependent Order Of Really Meek And Timid Souls." While on a behavioral level "meek and timid" are quite socially acceptable, it sadly lends itself to be taken advantage of--- if you can't turn on your aggressive or assertive styles when needed. Psychologically, passive people violate their rights and in doing so, teach other people how to hurt them in the future. That, unfortunately, creates a "victim mentality."

Their thinking reflects, "I'm not good enough."
Their words reflect, "I can't."
Their actions reflect – Silence.

The Aggressive – This is also the dominant pattern of someone with a severely damaged self-esteem. Psychologically, aggressive people violate everyone's rights without regard to circumstance or outcome. They usually display a healthy

"Weapons of Mass Instruction"

arrogance notable as an inflated sense of self-importance about condition or status. However, this arrogance is simply a cover-up for many insecurities. Also known as bullies, this personality style can be instrumental in particular threatening or hostile situations. However, it is the least socially accepted of all three.

Their thinking reflects, "I'm better than you."
Their words reflect, "You make me angry."
Their actions reflect – Shouting.

The Assertive – This is the dominant pattern of someone with a very high self-esteem. They are the most socially accepted of all three styles because they promote everyone's rights simultaneously. Assertive behavior respects the needs and rights of all individuals or parties. Instead of arrogance, they display pride, also known as a healthy sense of your dignity.

Their thinking reflects, "We're all important."
Their words reflect, "I believe we can."
Their actions reflect – Calm.

This type of "unity thinking" allows them to be accepted and successful in all areas due to a high level of trust. People want to associate and do business with them because they make you feel safe and secure.

To develop a more assertive personality, you must first establish three "sub" behaviors. Sub-behaviors are the foundation and substance of assertiveness.

1. Courage – The courage to stand up for yourself and others while effectively managing your boundaries. Courage is feeling fear, yet choosing to act.

2. Connection – The ability to positively influence people and move them to "win-win" outcomes through motivation, not manipulation or fear. Capacity to let people know you are on their side through thick and thin.

3. Caring – This is done with eye contact, smiling, sharing, being true to your word, and helping those who can't help themselves.

"Weapons of Mass Instruction"

Weapon # 33

3 Power Steps for Giving Constructive Criticism!

My first job after graduating from college was at the Federal Home Loan Bank in New York City. I worked there for two years on the 103rd floor of the World Trade Center. Three months into my employment at the bank, I received my first performance review. Despite the fact that my first three months were relatively successful, I was also responsible for some significant screw-ups which I contributed to a learning curve. Therefore, as the day of my "first ever" review approached, I was very nervous and anxious.

The actual review took about 30 minutes. My supervisor discussed my past performances, talked about goals for the future, and finally gave me a minimal list of what he called, "things to be aware of." I believe this was a euphemism for "constructive criticism." He never said one negative thing about my screw-ups or my learning curve. In fact, at one point it almost sounded as if he was complimenting my errors. He had a way of making my successes seem broad and my mistakes small or insignificant.

I walked out of my first review feeling empowered, feeling good about myself, ready to move on to larger projects, and with a raise in pay. I'll remember that day forever. It has shaped the manner in which I deal with employees, clients, customers, my children, and serves as the foundation for the **"3 Power Steps for Giving Constructive Criticism."**

It's not always easy giving criticism to others, especially if it's a loved one. However, if you follow the three easy steps described below, I'm sure you'll find that the experience can be rewarding and sometimes a fun opportunity.

Step One – Save their Face.

Here is a very fundamental and essential step. Despite the fact that the person has warranted a criticism session, your job is to build their self-esteem and make them

"Weapons of Mass Instruction"

look good unless you're dealing with severe and dangerous behavioral issues. When you are criticizing another, it is your job to approach the situation as if you are their coach, teacher or mentor, not a judge and jury. You must come with the mindset of helping--- not belittling. Avoid negative, destructive phrases such as:

"No one in the history of this company has screwed up like this."

"Only an idiot can make a mistake like this."

"Your heart was in the right place, but your brain was out to lunch."

"This company must be flypaper for idiots."

"I see the screw-up fairy has revisited us."

Your job is **not** to rub their face in the mistake and make them feel worse than they already do. There is nothing worse than kicking someone when they are already down and out. You can save their face and help them look good by opening the session with positive, constructive phrases such as:

"Don't feel bad, I made the same mistake once."

"This could have happened to anyone."

"Relax, we'll work on it together and create a solution."

"It's fine; let's just re-clarify your responsibilities."

I am sold on the fact that a significant part of the communication process is to help people feel better about themselves. Since you are the person about to deliver the critical blow, you have a tremendous opportunity and obligation to help that person change their behavior or correct their problem thru the process of construction— not destruction. This mindset will create trust, rapport, and credibility on your end, while the person on the receiving end basks in the comfort of your impeccable people skills.

"Weapons of Mass Instruction"

When you open a criticism session by saving someone's face, the rest of the process will flow quite smoothly, because the person will relax and drop their guard. When someone drops their guard or lowers their defenses, you'll find them in the perfect, receptive state of mind for step two.

Step Two – State Your Future Intention or what's Expected.

Now that you've constructively explained the problem or situation at hand thru the creative art of face-saving, it's now time to explain what behaviors are expected in the future. That is called the future intention or plan for behavior correction. Since the person is now relaxed and has dropped their defenses, you'll notice they are very receptive and eager to listen. The process has not hurt them so far, so they'll be ready to hear more of what you have to say.

Future Intentions for Behavior Modification Must Include 4 Steps:

1. The future intention must be specific.
2. The person must thoroughly understand what you are asking.
3. The person must have the ability to carry out the intention or goal—long term.
4. In business cases, the intention must be in writing. (Remember: if it's not in writing, it never happened.)

As an example, a real future intention might sound like this:

"Now that we've completely discussed the issue and you understand its consequences, here's what we expect from you in the future (fill in the blank). Since this was a trap that anyone could have fallen into, I'm sure it won't happen again, and we look forward to more great work from you."

Step Three – Thank Them & End It!

That's right! Thank them for listening and then end it—never bring it up again (unless the situation warrants it). It's imperative that you demonstrate your trust in the person and their ability to carry thru. Avoid monitoring their every move.

"Weapons of Mass Instruction"

Avoid looking over their shoulder watching or waiting for another mistake. That will make you crazy and them paranoid. They are now acutely aware of the problem; they have a plan to correct it, now it's time to let go and tend to new issues.

Let's Remember:

1. Save their face.
2. Building another's self-esteem during a criticism session is the sign of a master with extraordinary people skills.
3. State your future intentions or expectations.
4. Your future expectations must be specific, clearly understood, and put in writing.
5. Thank them and end it!
6. Avoid watching and scrutinizing your team or staff like a school monitor.

Quote for Thought:

"Criticism from a friend is better than flattery from an enemy." – Don Rickles

"Weapons of Mass Instruction"

Weapon # 34

3 Power Steps for Responding to Criticism!

In my entire career, I have never met anyone who enjoyed criticism. Have you ever been unjustly criticized? Worse, have you ever been criticized by a blatant imbecile who has the people skills of a brain-damaged Neanderthal? I've met many of these.

The truth is that receiving criticism can provide valuable feedback positively altering the quality of your life and career. Criticism is an insightful tool that can put you on a higher road, save you time, enhance your career, and prevent you from making mistakes that could be career damaging. Although we may not always like what we hear; learning to respond with grace and dignity to criticism can help us build a solid character. In my corporate seminars, I teach the attendees **"3 Power Steps for Responding to Criticism."** The purpose of these actions is to help you use criticism to your advantage, rather than it dragging you through the valley of embarrassment and self-pity.

Step One - Become a Student.

It is imperative for you to remember and continually focus on the fact that when you are being criticized, you *become a student.* Apparently, you are about to learn something about yourself or your behavior that you were not aware of earlier, and you need to adopt the attitude of a student. You are about to learn something that can help you in the future. If you always keep in mind that the information you are about to receive can help you, it will be less likely that you'll get upset, angry or defensive. Remember, becoming angry, defensive, or self-justifying, only teaches your critic where your weaknesses are and how to hurt or upset you again in the future. Merely SHUT UP and POLITELY LISTEN WITHOUT INTERRUPTION!

"Weapons of Mass Instruction"

Step Two - Politely Respond.

After your critic has had their say, then it is your turn to respond politely. That can be done by simply paraphrasing back to the person what you think you've just heard and how you feel about it. That is the perfect time to explain the reasons for your behavior or lapse in judgment. If you have unintentionally hurt someone, it's also the ideal time for an apology. Keep focusing on your breathing and remaining calm. Clenching your fists or grinding your teeth is also not recommended. Keep your eye contact gentle and even **thank them for bringing this valuable information to your attention.** Simply saying, *"Thank you very much for bringing this to my attention,"* can work wonders giving you that professional edge.

Step Three - State Your Future Intentions.

Now that you've heard and politely acknowledged your critic, the most professional way to terminate the discussion is to state your positive future intentions. That can be a short, polite chat on how you'll utilize the newly disclosed information for everyone's benefit. Remember, revealing your future intention is an acknowledgment that you have fully understood the criticism, and you are planning to make the necessary changes to the very best of your ability. It's important however that you do not fall into the trap of promising something that you cannot deliver. Be sure your future intention helps to resolve the issue and is something with which you can take immediate action.

Let's Remember:

1. Become a student.
2. Politely respond.
3. State your future intentions.

Quote for Thought:

"Most people don't object to criticism if it's favorable." – Lucille Ball

"Weapons of Mass Instruction"

Weapon # 35

De-Clutter Yourself!

Do you need to put on protective gear before you open your closets at home? Do you fear openning your desk at work? Is the paperwork on your desk disorganized and not current? If you answered "Yes" to any of these questions, there is a particular "term" for you.

But First, Here's More:

1. Do you save magazines, junk mail, advertisements and articles for the day you'll have time to read them?
2. Do you regularly misplace essential papers or bills?
3. Do you feel like you never have enough space?
4. Are you always searching for things on your desk?
5. Is your "inbox" piled so high you can ski on it?

If so, these are symptoms that you are: "Manic-Messy," "Debris-Dysfunctional," "Disorderly Orderly," "Untidy-Widey," and "Organizationally Challenged." However, the more acceptable terminology is a "Clutter-Bug."

Now let's get serious! Clutter in your home, office or desk space can be a valid stressor.

"Chronic clutter in our lives has a dramatic effect on us physiologically and psychologically."

I've had clients tell me that their clutter leaves them confused and disoriented. Others have said their clutter negatively affects their productivity. Others have said their clutter has caused them to lose focus and decreases their energy levels.

Some people have mastered the art of being organized, yet others have only mastered the art of being neat. The term "neat" means things are tidy but disorganized. The term "organized" means things are in order, but sloppy. A clutter-free lifestyle is created through the marriage of neat & organized.

"Weapons of Mass Instruction"

"Neat + Organized = Clutter Free"

I don't want to mislead you by saying that you can be clutter free overnight. However, the following tips are like an antibiotic to destroy the clutter-bug. If you apply the following weapons and stick with them, you will eventually notice a permanent end to clutter-bug infestation.

What to Do:

Step 1 – Clean and Clear off Your Desk at the End of Each Day.

That is a perfect way to end your day and begin the day after. A clear desk at the end of the day fills you with a sense of accomplishment, and a clear desk first thing the next morning gives you the feeling of a fresh start. Remember a messy desk is a sign of a messy mind.

Step 2 – Be Choosy About What You Keep.

Many people are afraid to toss things out for fear they may need it someday. However, with the internet and eBay, almost everything except sentimental objects can be replaced should you ever desperately need them again. Therefore, throw out or Ebay whatever you no longer use—it'll be worth it. I always first try to eBay the items in my clutter pile before I throw them out. Just ask yourself, *"Can this be easily replaced if I need it ten years from now?"* If the answer is "Yes,"---toss it! Also, be aware of recreational shopping, this can cause tons of clutter and money wasted. Never go shopping unless you need something. You will be amazed that you can do more--- with less.

Step 3 – When You Start Something---Complete It.

There's nothing more uncomfortable to me than having several incomplete assignments on my desk; it creates tons of blinding clutter. Multitasking is supposed to help you get things done faster, but when you try to juggle too many projects at once; ---everything in your life ends up incomplete. So if you're trying to simplify your life, simplify your approach to getting organized. I resolved this

"Weapons of Mass Instruction"

issue by deciding not to move on to another project until I completed the task at hand. I do not consider a project completed until it is over, finished, put away, out of sight and out of mind. I never leave any scraps of a project behind. Scraps turn into piles and piles turn into clutter.

Step 4 – Put Things Away, Re-file Quickly.

That is a significant habit to develop---just put things away. The moment you're finished with a file—re-file it in its proper place. Don't be a paper shuffler. Merely decide immediately to put your stuff away--- and do it. If you have any out of date emails or documents, shred or recycle them each week. Always open your mail by the trash, so you can quickly dispose of anything you will not read again.

Step 5 – Keep Frequently Used Items Within Your Reach.

Honestly, how much time do you waste looking for misplaced items? That is a significant key for being organized. This easy step can save you lots of time because you won't always be searching for things. That also comes in handy if you're pressed for time or meeting a deadline. Essential items such as a stapler, calculator, computer mouse, tape, and eyeglasses are always right within reach on my desk. Everything else is in its correct spot within the desk drawers.

Step 6 – Visualize a Productive Day.

Visualization has always been an essential part of my life. I use it to create a blueprint of my day, and for visualizing my goals completed. I use it to picture my life clutter-free—neat and clean. As I mentioned earlier, my ritual is to take 2-3 minutes in the morning and visualize exactly how I'd like my day to turn out. It's another powerful tool that when used regularly can positively affect your clutter infestation.

The ultimate goal for clutter bug elimination is to hoard less stuff while keeping everything in a productive, organized, and neat order. Bear in mind that remaining

"Weapons of Mass Instruction"

clutter-free for life is similar to motivation and bathing; it's something you need to do and keep up with daily.

Let's Remember:

1. Clean off your desk at the end of each day.
2. Be choosy about what you keep.
3. Finish everything you start.
4. When you're finished, put everything away in its proper place quickly.
5. Things may be "finished," but they **are not** "complete" until you put them away.
6. Keep frequently used items within your reach.
7. Visualize a productive day.

Quote for Thought:

"Out of clutter, find simplicity." — Albert Einstein

"Weapons of Mass Instruction"

Weapon # 36

Business Advice from the Godfather!

"The Godfather" is undeniably one of the greatest films in cinematic history. It was written by Mario Puzo, directed by Francis Ford Coppola, and released in 1972. This theatrical masterpiece tells the story of the fictional mafia crime family known as the "Corleone's."

I was only 11 years old at the time this film was released. Even at that young age my buddies and I enjoyed our favorite pastime which was quoting lines from the Godfather. Coincidently, it was also a favorite pastime for many adults. I cannot tell you how many times I've watched the film and its sequels because I have lost count. What I can say, however, is that the Godfather contains many great one-liners, sound bites, or quotes that can be applied directly to your business. Even if you are not running an organized crime family, these movie quotes can be applied to any business or life situation.

For years I taught a popular half-day seminar entitled, "The Godfather Speaks." I explained the following 16 principles direct from the Godfather trilogy. The response and success stories from my attendees were so overwhelming that I'd like to share them here with you.

Let's go through all 16; let's see how many of these quotes you remember, and then take a moment to discover how to apply them.

1. "Don't hate your enemies, it affects your judgment."

And if your judgment is impaired, you'll do stupid things. How many of us are guilty of this? Take extra caution in how you treat or talk about your competition. Different types of sarcasm, ridicule, and jealousy will dull your mind and stifle your creative juices. That can drastically impede your progress and destroy years of hard work as you try to remain in the forefront of your industry.

"Weapons of Mass Instruction"

2. "Try to think what people around you think."

That helps you remain ahead of the competition and to know what your customer wants even before they know it. It allows you to imagine what it's like to be in their skin and view the world through their perceptions. That is a significant strategy and has been the backbone of every successful business success in human history. It's not so much about being psychic, but instead about the power to carefully plot trends and predict future needs by viewing the world through your customer's eyes. Let this remind you of Steve Jobs.

3. "Just don't say you're innocent; it insults my intelligence."

Taking responsibility for your actions and the actions of your company are the backbone of a healthy character. Managers or supervisors without character rarely succeed long-term. We are not always responsible for all the things that happen to us, but we are responsible for how we act when they do occur. We are also expected to own up to our mistakes. Remember, your moral fiber is a self-portrait. If you're not afraid to face the music, you may someday lead the band.

4. "Women and children can be careless, not men."

In today's marketplace, *everyone* must approach their day with care. There are no exceptions! Carelessness leads to forgetfulness which leads to sloppiness which leads to the destruction of careers.

5. "A man who doesn't spend time with his family can never be a real man."

Naturally, this quote speaks to ladies, too. It's a quote promoting the importance of balancing your business and personal life. According to research conducted at the University of California School of Medicine, *"Without life balance, most people will crash and severely burn-out."* Sadly, only 7% of the population is living the so-called "good life" that success promised. You must seek and find a balance, so you don't end up a statistic.

"Weapons of Mass Instruction"

6. "It's not personal; it's business."

Here is a master key to emotional control, conflict escalation, and dealing with difficult people. You must learn the art of separating business from personal issues. The two do not belong together. You're not even getting paid enough to take things personally---are you?

7. "Make them an offer they can't refuse."

In sales never ask yourself, *"How can I sell this customer my product?"* Instead ask, *"What can I do to earn your business?"* The answer is to make them an offer they can't refuse. Make them an offer that your competitor has not--- or cannot. When you make the offer, remain confident, excited, positive, and secure. When you make customers offers they can't refuse they tend to become more loyal.

8. "Never let anybody outside the family know what you're thinking."

Two great Biblical quotes reinforce the message contained in this principle; I mentioned them earlier:

1. *"Never tell your left hand what your right hand is doing."*

2. *"Go forth and tell no one."*

I summed up these principles in just two words earlier, and here we go again – *"SHUT UP!"* Never discuss personal business with anyone outside the family or your organization. Remember, *"Loose lips sink ships."*

9. "Hear bad news immediately."

Here is the motto of every great leader, supervisor, and manager. Hearing bad news immediately helps you to shift to the "save and recovery" mode quickly. Perhaps you can stop the problem before it causes more damage. Maybe you can brainstorm a creative solution before your customers or clients learn of the unfortunate circumstances. Worst case scenario it gives you ample time to get out of town before you get caught.

"Weapons of Mass Instruction"

10. "Don't ever take sides with anyone against the family."

I heard this principle when I was a young boy, except my mom used different terminology which was, *"Don't bite the hand that feeds you."* Taking sides against your family or your company is a quick way to create bad blood and end up sleeping on the couch--- or with the fishes. Once again, Michael Corleone was correct!

11. "I have always believed helping your fellow man is profitable in every sense, personally and bottom line."

The great motivator Zig Ziglar taught, *"You can always get what you want if you just help enough other people get what they want."* That's a personal and professional fact! If the first thought in your mind as you awaken every morning is, *"How many people can I help today,"* you're on the right track to succeed. I have found in my life that the more people I help, the more people want to help me. That is the basis of the law of reciprocity.

12. "Our ships must all sail in the same direction."

The only way to achieve this is through the power of a mutually agreed upon mission statement. Your mission statement must indicate where you are going and in what direction you choose to get there. Your goals, values, principles, ethics, morals, and ideals must coincide for a business relationship to thrive and prosper.

13. "This I cannot do."

This great principle teaches us to "Know Thyself!" You must know yourself, and you must know your limits. Truly successful people know when they are out of their league. They know how to surround themselves with other experts in the field, and they know how to delegate. Unless you wear a red cape with a large "S" on your chest, it's okay to acknowledge weaknesses and seek support by sending in your troops.

"Weapons of Mass Instruction"

14. "I want reliable people; people that aren't gonna be carried away."

Isn't that what every business wants? The critical point to remember here is that employees are only as good as their managers. Managers are only as good as their supervisors. And supervisors are only as good as the CEO. Remember that a dead fish rots from the head down. If you want reliable people—then train middle and upper management.

15. "You never know when you're going to have to feed a crowd, so make sure you know how to cook."

You also never know if you're going to be challenged by a customer, or confronted by a supervisor, or caught in the middle of a cross-fire. This quote is a lesson in preparedness. An opportunity has the uncanny habit of favoring those who have paid the price of years of preparation. Today's preparation determines tomorrow's achievements. Keep your eyes open, the oven on, and the table set.

16. "Make your peace."

The perfect way to end your day is to leave your job knowing you've done your best. You put in a good day's work, and you're proud of your accomplishments. Now it's time to peacefully let it go so you can have the opportunity to start fresh. That is a key in maintaining your psychological health and edge.

Quote for Thought:

"Everything I learned I learned from the movies." - Audrey Hepburn

"Weapons of Mass Instruction"

"Two Seas of Palestine"

By Bruce Barton

There are two seas in the Palestine. One is fresh, and fish are in it. Splashes of green adorn its banks. Trees spread their branches over it and stretch out their thirsty roots to sip of its healing waters.

The River Jordan makes this sea with sparkling water from the hills. So it laughs in the sunshine. And men build their houses near to it, birds build their nests, and every kind of life is happier because it is there.

The River Jordan flows on south into another sea. Here is no splash of fish, no fluttering leaf, no song of birds, no children's laughter. Travelers choose another route, unless on urgent business. The air hangs heavy above its water, and neither man nor beast nor fowl will drink.

What makes this mighty difference in these two neighboring seas? Not the River Jordan. It empties the same good water into both. Not the soil in which they lie; not the country round about.

This is the difference. The Sea of Galilee receives but does not keep the Jordan. For every drop that flows into it another drop flows out. The giving and receiving go on in equal measure. The other sea is shrewder, hoarding its income jealousy. It will not be tempted into any generous impulse. Every drop it gets, it keeps.

The Sea of Galilee gives and lives. This other sea gives nothing. It is named the Dead!

There are two seas in Palestine, and there are two kinds of people and businesses in this world.

Which are you?

"Weapons of Mass Instruction"

About the Author

John Eric Jacobsen is the Co-founder and President of Jacobsen Business Seminars, Inc. John has consulted for more than 1,000 companies and addressed more than 1,000,000 people in 5,000 talks and seminars throughout the US. As a keynote speaker and seminar leader, he addresses many people each year. **(http://www.JohnEricJacobsen.com/)**

John speaks to corporate and public audiences on the subjects of Personal and Professional Development, including the executives and staff of many of America's largest corporations and our own United States Military. John is also the co-author of the fantastic book, "Conversations on Customer Service & Sales," and the ground-breaking, "The Jesus Lecture."

His exciting talks and seminars on Leadership, Conflict Resolution, Self-Esteem, Goal Achievement, Communication Mastery, and Success Psychology bring about immediate changes and long-term results.

Also, a practicing Hypnotherapist, John is the founder and author of the Kids in Trance Program. This unique, beneficial program teaches parents how to use clinical hypnotherapy with their kids/teens for problem-solving and mental development. **(KidsInTrance.com)**

Clients Include:

United States Army, United States Marines, United States Department of Chemical Defense, United Defense, Pepsi Cola, Alcon Surgical Laboratories, Subaru of America, Lourdes Medical Center, Comcast, Corning Inc., AT&T, Federal Home Loan Bank, GPU Energy, West Virginia University and Norwest Mortgage.

Please follow us on Twitter & FaceBook – Thanks!

Made in the USA
Las Vegas, NV
22 April 2024